SUCCESSFUL
PRODUCT
MANAGEMENT

MARKETING IN ACTION SERIES

SUCCESSFUL PRODUCT MANAGEMENT

Second Edition

A Guide to Strategy, Planning and Development

STEPHEN MORSE

KOGAN PAGE

YOURS TO HAVE AND TO HOLD

BUT NOT TO COPY

First published in 1994
Second edition 1998

Kogan Page Limited
120 Pentonville Road
London N1 9JN

British Library Cataloguing in Publication Data

A CIP record for this book is available from the British Library.

ISBN 0 7494 2702 7

Typeset by JS Typesetting, Wellingborough, Northants.
Printed in Great Britain by Biddles Ltd, Guildford and King's Lynn.

Contents

Marketing in Action Series

Series Editor: Norman Hart

In producing this series, the advice and assistance has been sought of a prestigious editorial panel representing the principal professional bodies, trade associations and business schools.

The Series Editor for the Marketing in Action books is Norman Hart who is a writer of some ten books himself. He currently runs his own marketing consultancy, and is also an international lecturer at marketing and other such conferences as well as the leading business schools.

ALSO IN THIS SERIES

Creative Effective Marketing Communications, Daniel Yadin
The Effective Use of Sponsorship, David Wragg
Getting the Best from Agencies (and Other Outside Services),
    Geoffrey Smith
How to Produce Successful Advertising, A D Farbey
A Practical Guide to Marketing Communications, Tom Brannan

Preface

My friend says she never reads the preface until she's finished the book; she doesn't want to spoil the plot – even in the Second edition!

Nevertheless there are a couple of things which should be set down before you get to Chapter 1. First, the book is designed for newly appointed product managers or those who want to freshen their ideas. I have found that many books on marketing give an occasional nod in the direction of product managers, but do not accept that he (or she) is often the architect and support of the product line.

With that in mind the book outlines the product manager's role and function, provides precepts and tips on strategy, has some words to say about new product development and rounds it off with some thoughts on effectiveness.

It is not a novel. It does not need to be read from beginning to end. It tries to be a 'top-right-hand-drawer' book – to be referred to when the reader wants to remind himself (or herself) what steps he or she should take to solve a problem.

If you recognise thoughts and ideas which have their origins with other writers, I have not wittingly stolen them. Over the years I have acquired many ideas from both writers and practitioners, whose sources I have now no way of acknowledging accurately (if at all!). Those unacknowledged must, please, accept my apologies.

But I must most gratefully acknowledge the help of Anne Waites in the hard grind of typing the manuscript, and the work of Hilary Condron of JWP on the diagrams and tables.

The next stage after reading the book is to try to apply those ideas you find useful to your own situation. Perhaps it might help to read some of the books in the Bibliography.

Good luck with your product line!

1

The Need for Product Management

INTRODUCTION

The following quotations are from advertisements for product managers. They demonstrate that the product management system is alive and well. This book is aimed at helping these four newly appointed product managers and all those who are bearing the burdens and heat of the day in the product manager function. The job descriptions quoted could well serve as a 'text' for the book.

> We need someone who not only can analyse the market for X but identify opportunities for new and existing products and develop the resulting spec and rationale. To do this successfully you must be able to isolate the factors which influence the market such as customer needs, product applications, installation practice and environmental issues.

The position

– Manage range of Y products. Achieve sales and profile targets. Report to marketing manager.
– Monitor market trend and product development. Develop supplier relationships.
– Liaise effectively across functional disciplines. Motivate and manage small team.

Growth in the UK has been outstanding . . . Aggressive marketing is fundamental to success . . . To further develop the potential . . . a new

Product Manager is required . . . With a knowledge of the 'Z' market and at least 5 years product management experience you will be a proven 'Product Champion' . . . You will need strategic marketing and team leadership skills as well as being an expert negotiator with good communications ability at all levels.

The Product Manager will control a portfolio of innovative products, working with sales, marketing and development staff to ensure maximum profitability and exploitation of the portfolio through the development and execution of demanding business plans, often taking products to new market sectors . . . You will have a strong feel for business and work well in a multi-disciplined team.

So far as I can discover, very few books have been written about product management. There are many books about marketing, marketing strategy and analysis, marketing planning and marketing implementations (some of these are included in the Bibliography at the end of the book). Mentions are made of the function of the product manager. Often only the pitfalls of the product management system are discussed.

There are large numbers of product managers. Often these are new to the principles and processes of marketing. Often their responsibilities are extensive and expectations of their performance overwhelming. It seems only fair, therefore, to provide them with a book which discusses the theory and practice of product management, which focuses exclusively on what the product manager needs to know and what skills the product manager needs to fulfil his/ her function.

[*Note:* Today, I would guess that more than 50 per cent of product managers are female. To ensure that neither men nor women feel excluded I propose to alternate 'he' and 'she', in successive chapters. This means that, in referring to a product manager, 'he' would include 'she' and 'she' would include 'he'.]

STARTING POINTS FOR THE SYSTEM

Envisage a business with a single product or service. Starting at the 'creation' stage and going through to the 'customer satisfaction stage', each function has only to deal with a single product or service. Every process is geared to ensuring that the service or product is produced, is presented to the customer and provides satisfaction. The organisation structure of the business is geared to these integrated objectives.

Now envisage a business with a number of different products or services. Two things will have happened.

1. More specialisation at each stage of the process – R&D separate from production; packaging and distribution, market research, merchandising and price in separate sections; sales, advertising, sales promotion and after-sales services all separately managed.
2. Increased need for co-ordination, management, prioritisation and control among the different functions of the business.

It is always held that the product management system started with Procter and Gamble in the late 1920s. One product was not doing well and a manager was assigned to give that product (Camay soap) his full attention. Other product managers followed this successful innovation. Thus the 'brand manager' was born.

Perhaps a clearer illustration of the development of the product manager is shown in the history of the Manchester textile industry (the 'cotton trade'). The process is (roughly) as follows:

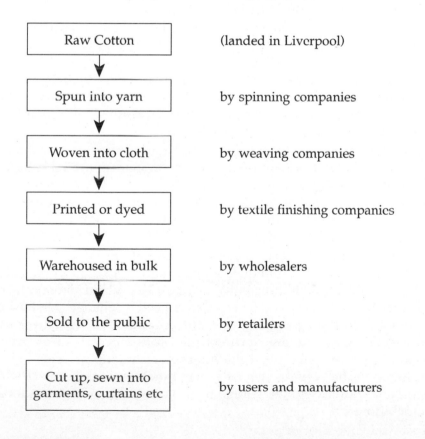

Raw Cotton	(landed in Liverpool)
Spun into yarn	by spinning companies
Woven into cloth	by weaving companies
Printed or dyed	by textile finishing companies
Warehoused in bulk	by wholesalers
Sold to the public	by retailers
Cut up, sewn into garments, curtains etc	by users and manufacturers

The control over this process in the 1930s was in the hands of a 'converter' – often an individual with just an office and a telephone who managed the movement from raw cotton to the retail shops, making the appropriate decisions all down the line. When the process came into the hands of vertically organised companies the tasks of an independent 'converter' were taken over by a 'product manager'.

The first product managers, then, were co-ordinators – perhaps secretarial figures – rather than entrepreneurs. The latter function has been added later. Very much so in the cotton trade.

THE MARKETING CONCEPT AND THE SYSTEM

Further impetus was given to the need for product management when businesses began to embrace the 'marketing concept'.

In broad terms the marketing concept established the belief that all the activities of the business should be directed towards two parallel goals – fulfilling customer requirements and making a profit. Businesses were pushed gradually into this way of thinking because of:

1. advances in technology in their industries (eg television sets moving from valves to transistors);
2. development of new raw materials as substitutes (eg carbon fibre for steel, plastics for leather etc);
3. new sources of labour (eg cheaper manufacture in low labour cost countries) and capital (eg freer movement of capital between countries);
4. expanding markets (eg development of the European Common Market, markets in the USA and on the Pacific Rim).

These all led to the need to change or modify existing products – both in production techniques and in market acceptance; fashion changes became more frequent and affected a much wider spectrum of products and services. There was a need to change persuasion methods; an illustration of this is the enormous increase over the last 20 years in the use of direct mail (often described as direct marketing) fax, e-mail and the Internet. Changing markets led to changes in distribution channels, new points of direct contact with potential purchasers (eg garage forecourt shops and international exhibitions).

DEVELOPMENT OF MARKETING PLANNING

There has also been a greater interest in marketing planning (see Malcolm McDonald's books). When marketing plans are to be made there is a need to tie together products and markets. There is a need to conceive more imaginative ways of developing the business through:

- research and forecasting;
- establishing strategies;
- planning the marketing mix;
- budgeting revenue and cost;
- scheduling activities;
- setting up controls;

and relating these general functions to a specific product destined for a particular market.

In consumer goods companies the emphasis seems to be on packaging, pricing and promotion. Thus there has developed a pretty clear task of 'brand manager'. (For brand managers there exist a number of straightforward 'how to' books, such as Davidson or Phillips. They all illustrate a specialised aspect of the product management system. See Chapter 9.)

With industrial products and services the drive towards better marketing planning has led to the need to base plans not only on the quantitative aspects of the market but also on the product's qualitative impact. Identification of the different needs of users, buyers and decision makers has led to closer examination of the impact of the 'controllable factors' in the marketing mix. Chapter 7 describes a method of assessing the appropriate action to influence the customer's decision-making process.

WHERE THE PRODUCT MANAGEMENT SYSTEM CAN BE EFFECTIVE

The original (and logical) basis for a product management system was the thought that 'we have the products, we had better see that they are managed properly'. The business which had an organisation structure with powerful operating sections would have found the product management system a necessary improvement.

Take, for example, a large insurance company. Its engine is the whole administrative machine processing premiums and claims, looking after members' affairs. It also has two other major sections – a sales section, which often consists of independent agents; and a product development unit, responsible for creating new forms of insurance to fit today's new risks. A product management system became necessary to tie together the output of operating divisions so as to provide a service which fitted customer requirements (qv marketing concept).

I have devised question and answer sections which may help to clarify the position.

Would the system improve a situation where there are a number of product ranges, all being sold through the same outlets and the marketing manager has a large staff including marketing planning, advertising and market research departments?
Yes, because each product range currently is given a different priority by each department in marketing. Appointing product managers would ensure that each range was given full weight both within the company and in the market.

Would a product management system be better than simply hiving off each product line into a separate division with its own dedicated production, marketing and sales?
Yes, because the chances are that the overheads of a partitioned business could well be too heavy for individual product lines to bear.

Wouldn't the system make it difficult to 'kill off' unprofitable products?
No, because the product management set-up would clearly identify the costs, revenue and profitability of each product manager's 'line'.

What are the pitfalls of introducing the system?
According to Kotler there are three:

1. the system introduces many sources of conflict and frustration;
2. the product manager becomes an expert in his product but does not have the chance of becoming expert in the marketing functions (or vice versa);
3. the system turns out to be costlier than first thought because of the proliferation of assistants and specialists.

It seems to me that with some forethought most of the pitfalls can be avoided.

How can you ensure that the product management system is successful? There are five golden rules:

1. *Ensure that the system is suitable for the situation.* There is no point in introducing product managers into a simple structure with, say, one product line and one market or into a situation where the whole business has been decentralised. In both cases the product manager function is unnecessary.
2. *Assign an appropriate role to the product manager.* If the user's need is highly technical then the relationship should be an intimate one with the 'producer' (designer, manufacturing manager, etc) and a product manager can add nothing. His/her role should be to facilitate direct contact.
3. *Ensure that those chosen to be product managers are sufficiently qualified.* The system cannot function successfully if the 'communication centre' lacks weight. Salespeople, production staff, marketing specialists must have the confidence that the product manager listens to their point of view and takes account of their views in planning action.
4. *Top management must support the system.* The product manager must not be bypassed or ignored by senior managers going direct to operating managers, particularly in a crisis!
5. *Top managers should have realistic expectations of the success of the product management system.* The installation of the product management system cannot (and should not be expected to) produce immediate results. Depending on the culture of the business (which often has to do with the age and length of service of senior managers) it will take 12 to 18 months to see any major improvement. Improved profitability will occur as a result of the willingness to co-operate and the ability of the new product managers to *plan*, to communicate and to listen.

The role and function of product managers is discussed in detail in Chapter 2. The job descriptions show that from originally being 'product led', the function of the product manager is (largely) the interpretation of the market's requirements and is thus now 'market led'.

2

The Role of the Product Manager

The product management concept provides for a managerial focus on products or brands as profit-generating systems – while at the same time allowing for flexibility in the role of the product manager and in her position in the organisation. Generalisations of this kind do not help the practising product manager in her search after the 'nitty-gritty' of the function. Nor does the following quotation:

> The brand or product managers continue to be responsible for the day-to-day marketing operations and problems associated with their products and provide assistance and advice to the marketing manager and others on these when the annual tactical plans are being prepared.
>
> *Douglas W. Foster (1972) Planning for Products and Markets*

FUNCTION DESCRIPTIONS

In addition to the necessarily sketchy descriptions given in the recruitment advertisement in Chapter 1, here are some which outline the 'basics' of the function of product managers in three different kinds of business.

First an illustration of the function description of a product manager in a fast-moving consumer goods (fmcg) company selling (say) detergents, sweets, packaged foods, etc:

Her objective:

To maximise the contribution of brand X to the company's profits.

Her tasks:

1. Creating an annual product plan for brand X (see Chapter 3 for details of a product plan).
2. Making a forecast of sales by market area.
3. Discussing the forecast with production; agreeing on output levels to fit the product plan.
4. Arranging packaging, design, quantities, types (new packs, packs for special events etc).
5. Recommending a communication strategy and having discussions with advertising, sales etc.
6. Arranging an advertising budget, planning promotion, making contact with advertising agencies.
7. Proposing and planning promotional 'deals' – 'in', to encourage stocking by retail, and 'out', movement off the shelf.
8. Discussing matters with sales management and key accounts.
9. Establishing/agreeing pricing and discounts.
10. Putting together and agreeing budgets of:
    – volume;
    – sales revenue;
    – orders;
    – product costs;
    – profit.
11. Planning market research, briefing agencies.
12. Setting up controls to monitor performance.
13. Maintaining regular reviews with production, promotion and sales operations.

Note how this function description fits with the common view of 'marketing'. Responsibility starts in the warehouse, after the product has been produced. Discussions about the specification of the product are not part of the product manager's responsibility. Quite often, in fact, the product manager is expected to deal only with advertising and sales promotion. She has to deal with senior and experienced operational managers from both production and sales.

Second, an illustration of a typical industrial product manager's function description:

Her objective:

To maximise profit on the product line. (Note the difference with the brand manager, who has only to maximise the contribution of the brand to the company's profits.)

Her tasks:

1. Establishing basic specifications for the product (and changes thereto).
2. Producing a product plan (see Chapter 3 for an outline of the plan).
3. Making forecasts of product quantities per customer group, per month.
4. Interpreting forecasts into monthly production orders.
5. Setting pricing strategies and levels of prices.
6. Agreeing budgets of volume, revenue, costs and profit.
7. Agreeing with the sales department the approach to customers.
8. Ensuring contact with sales administration (eg in relation to customer queries/complaints)
9. Formulating communication strategy and organising advertising and sales promotion.
10. Organising, planning and interpreting research into the market.
11. Discussing innovation with R&D.
12. Discussing production possibilities with production.
13. Arranging packaging, warehousing and physical distribution.
14. Evaluating existing distribution agencies (wholesalers, distributors, agents etc).
15. Initiating discussion on future strategies.
16. Setting up controls to monitor performance.
17. Arranging annual reviews.

(Note the basic difference between the industrial product manager and her brand manager counterpart lies in the extent of her responsibility. The tasks extend from the product specification to the customer's satisfaction.)

Third, an illustration of the function of a no less important member of the product manager family: the product manager in a branch of an international or multinational company. Typically this individual would be the local product manager in a country where the multinational had customers and perhaps some production but whose headquarters were elsewhere. Cross-border acquisition has made this circumstance more common in the last decade.

Her objective:

To maximise sales of product line or lines in the market for which she is responsible. (Note that for this product manager the responsibility is to maximise sales. In a multinational organisation the responsibility for profit is taken by the central staff.)

Her tasks:

1. Undertake market research in order to estimate quantities required.
2. Make recommendations on how many outlets should be used – what type of outlet and how they should be approached (eg a pharmaceutical product manager would be concerned with outlets such as doctors, wholesalers, pharmacies, pharmacology departments in hospitals).
3. Forecast volumes per outlet.
4. Plan the packaging to fit the local market (eg translated into local language, fitting local legal requirements, in local pack sizes).
5. Establish (and agree) the local 'sales story'.
6. Discuss local selling and communication strategy.
7. Plan and organise advertising and promotion (or translate international advertisements)
8. Agree annual (quarterly, weekly) budgets of volume, value and cost and submit to head office via local manager.
9. Create a local market plan.
10. Set up monitoring, review and reporting procedures.

Looking at these, the aspiring product manager could well feel confused. Indeed, she might well suggest that her job is not like any of these 'typical' descriptions. She might well find that a serious approach to the tasks is inappropriate and that Karl Marx's view of history repeating itself 'the first time as tragedy, the second time as farce' might well be a more apt description.

Asked what the role of the product manager should be, respondents reply:

■ 'a little general manager';
■ 'an entrepreneur';
■ 'a co-ordinator of activities performed by others';
■ 'a clerk for the product's real managers – top management'.

It is worth pursuing this role problem further as it will help to determine the skills needed by product managers to fulfil their role.

THREE MAJOR ASPECTS

To counter the remarks above it is necessary to divide consideration of the product manager's role into three:

■ management tasks;
■ marketing decisions;
■ organisational points of view.

None of the following lists is definitive but they start from work done by Clewett and Stosch (1972) with packaged consumer goods product managers in the USA. [I have modified the list based on my own experience of industrial marketing managers in UK and Holland.]

First an attempt is made to identify those ten management tasks where the product manager might well (perhaps should!) play a major role. It is unlikely that she will have sole responsibility for anything except the communication of the product plan and the review of the plan.

Perhaps the best way to start is to make a questionnaire, so that you can tick the answers (in pencil!) as to whether in your case you have:

■ a sole responsibility (a);
■ a major role (b);
■ a minor role (c).

You should tick where appropriate.

		(a)	(b)	(c)
1.	Establishing marketing objectives for the product.	☐	☐	☐
2.	Planning marketing activities.	☐	☐	☐
3.	Agreeing product specification.	☐	☐	☐
4.	Planning monthly/annual volume/quantities.	☐	☐	☐
5.	Determining budgets of marketing costs.	☐	☐	☐
6.	Setting up controls to monitor activities.	☐	☐	☐
7.	Communicating the plans to 'operators'.	☐	☐	☐
8.	Monitoring progress to agreed results.	☐	☐	☐
9.	Specifying corrective action.	☐	☐	☐
10.	Supplying end-of-year report to 'management'.	☐	☐	☐

Second, drawing the line between 'management tasks' and 'marketing decisions' is somewhat arbitrary but it may clarify the product manager's functions. Which marketing decision areas do you have:

■ sole responsibility for (a);
■ play a major role in (b);
■ undertake a minor part only (c).

You should tick where appropriate.

	(a)	(b)	(c)
Marketing decisions with reference to:			
1. Product specification.	☐	☐	☐
2. Product quantities.	☐	☐	☐
3. Packaging, sizes, design.	☐	☐	☐
4. Pricing, including distribution margins.	☐	☐	☐
5. Communication theme.	☐	☐	☐
6. Choice of promotion media.	☐	☐	☐
7. Market research subjects.	☐	☐	☐
8. Market research budget.	☐	☐	☐
9. Promotion actions, type and timing.	☐	☐	☐
10. Instructions to salesforce.	☐	☐	☐
11. Instructions to agents/distributors.	☐	☐	☐
12. Sales targets.	☐	☐	☐
13. Selection/change of agents/distributors.	☐	☐	☐

Every product manager will have a different level of input into marketing decisions. Research has shown that in most companies she will be, for the most part, a 'recommender' or an 'influencer' of decisions. It is however the case that in industrial goods companies, the product manager will play a more responsible role. Her task will be more of an interpreter of market requirements, from details of product specifications to selection of distribution systems and outlets.

With the obvious difference that 'services' are intangible the functions of a (services) product manager (tasks, skills and responsibilities) seem to be broadly the same as those in 'industrial goods' businesses. Her concern is the delivery of services which fit customer requirements. The uncovering and stimulation of these requirements is part of the marketing function.

The third major aspect is that of organisational position. In conventional 'organigrams' the product manager is found in the marketing staff section – responsible perhaps to a product group manager. Something like the top half of Figure 2.1. Or she may find herself isolated, part of a decentralised division or strategic business unit (SBU), as shown in the lower half of Figure 2.1.

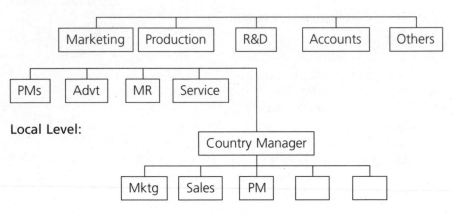

Figure 2.1 *Conventional organisation*

In either case the task is, in essence, to persuade all the other department decision makers to at least recognise the existence of your product. Thus the product manager has to steer her product through the 'rocks and rapids' of its progress from creation to customer satisfaction.

Part of the difficulty may well be overcome by using outside agencies to do the work of, say, market research or sales promotion or advertising. It is often easier for a product manager to persuade outside agencies to do her bidding than expecting departments inside the company to change their priorities for her!

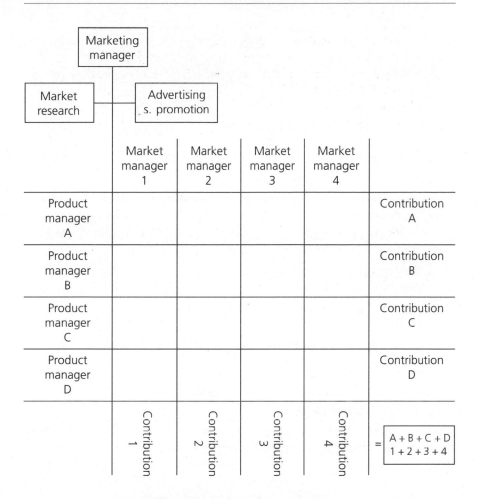

Figure 2.2 *Matrix structure*

One of the ways round this problem – and it must be admitted that all who have ever been product managers recognise it – is to arrange the organisation on a 'matrix' as shown in Figure 2.2. Clear lines of responsibility are shown. Product manager A is responsible for the 'contribution' of product A in all markets. (Similarly with product managers B, C and D.) Market managers (or sales managers with responsibilities covering identified markets) are responsible for 'contributions' of the customers in their market area, resulting from the sale of all products.

EXAMPLE

A company which manufactured and printed packaging had four major product lines:

■ printed card packages;
■ printed paper packaging;
■ printed plastic packaging;
■ bread wrappers etc and miscellaneous.

Each of these product lines was made the responsibility of a product manager, who was judged on the contribution made by her product. To balance this there happened to be four separate market areas which could be identified and managed, namely:

1. detergent and food manufacturers;
2. export;
3. northern region sales; and
4. southern region sales.

Each of these market areas was the responsibility of a market manager who was judged on the contribution of her customers.

The matrix shown in Figure 2.2 was established as the basis of the marketing organisation of the company. There were four important aspects:

1. The marketing manager had overall supervision of both product management and sales.
2. Specialised departments (market research and advertising) had their services 'requested' by product managers or market managers and final allocations were made by the marketing manager.
3. Each product manager and each market manager was under pressure to discuss and agree the content of specific plans for each product in each market.
4. Measurement of success was based on contribution and this was clearly defined as follows:

Total sales revenue (product or market)	xxxxx
Cost of goods sold (defined)	xxxx
Contribution I (gross profit)	xxx
Marketing expenses	xx
Contribution II	x
Sum of all Contribution IIs =	8x
Less overhead	xx
Net profit before tax	x

Each product manager and each market manager was assessed on Contribution I, their direct 'marketing' expenses and Contribution II.

Dominguez (1971) conceives of product management as a hexagon (Figure 2.3) where the items:

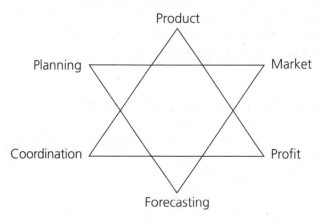

Figure 2.3 *Product management tasks*

create the necessary organisation position. It used to be said that a 'progress chaser' was an unnecessary function in a factory if everyone was doing her job properly. However, the difficulty is always the integration of, or consensus on, priorities. The product manager's input into organisation structures is to make them work more smoothly and more effectively.

Writing in *Business Marketing* in 1986 Robert H. Randolph summed up the product manager's responsibilities as follows:

- product strategy;
- product planning;
- product development monitoring;
- product marketing;
- product business activities (financial returns);

and suggested that the product manager (at least in advanced technology companies) would have the following interfaces:

- with top management (guidance and objectives);
- with finance (return on investment and budgets);
- with the legal department (over contracts);
- with sales;
- with design and engineering (product development);
- with production (manufacture);
- with marketing (marketing plans and strategies);

commenting, 'the product manager works with many different parts of the organisation, typically with responsibility that outstrips her authority. A product manager must understand the subtleties of exerting power and influence without apparent authority'.

Rather than create an authoritative checklist, I would ask you to check your own job description against the ideas in this chapter and answer the following questions:

■ Do you have clear objectives?
■ Are your interfaces understood by the different departments?
■ Are your responsibilities clear?
■ Can you bring authority to bear on situations where you are trying to influence other departments to fulfil the agreed plan?
■ Are there areas in the progress of the product from creation to customer which are no-go areas for you?
■ Do you receive sufficient information in both facts and figures to enable you to measure performance against plan?
■ Does your boss know your answers to these questions?

3

Developing the Product Plan: The Market

In spite of the 'job description' which, as a newly appointed product manager, you will have now put in the top right-hand drawer of your desk, there will be an expectation that you produce a product plan. Next week? So this chapter establishes the outline of the product plan and sets out to describe and discuss the first (and vital) chapter – the one about 'the market'.

THE SHAPE OF THE PRODUCT PLAN

Because the product plan is one of the major building blocks of the marketing plan, which in its turn is a major part of the business plan, it must follow a standard structure. Each business will devise its own. Here is a model which can apply to industrial goods companies and service organisations. (The assumption that a 'product' and a 'service' are interchangeable concepts is useful when trying to establish basic principles. To prove this, try applying the model to a hotel, an airline or a laundry service.)

THE MARKET BACKGROUND

Whatever the product manager is managing, whatever sort of product or product line, whatever kind of service, the first step in

EXAMPLE

Product plan shape

1. Background of the market and market segments:
    - size and shape – previous years
                    – expected next year;
    - own share – previous
                – expected;
    - main competition – changes.
2. Product range:
    - special features;
    - costs and profitability.
3. Distribution channels:
    - types;
    - discount structures;
    - make-to-order constraints;
    - stock levels.
4. Promotion recommendations:
    - outlets;
    - sales effort;
    - advertising plans;
    - promotion plans;
    - special efforts;
    - PR activities;
    - dealer support.
5. Sales revenue expected – *monthly*.
6. Marketing costs planned – *monthly*.
7. Contribution – *monthly*.
8. Controls:
    - market research requirement;
    - profit levels;
    - monthly assessments;
    - stock variance.
9. Action required by ....
                    ....
10. New product development:
    - product type;
    - development deadlines;
    - development costs.
11. Product creation:
    - market research;
    - R&D action.

planning is to look hard at the market. Sounds easy. Sounds straightforward and obvious. Only common sense. But very many businesses, from the largest to the smallest, from the National Health Service or the national airline to the sandwich counter down the street or the small garage, will normally begin by worrying about what they do, make, produce, offer; and only later think about who they are offering it to! So, look hard at the market!

The second mistake that is usually made is to consider the market as anyone within range. ('We sell to anyone who wants to buy', 'We offer our service in the marketplace for use by anyone who happens to want it' are typical comments by those who come to marketing for the first time.) Thus the product manager's skill starts with persuading those concerned with company strategy that marketing demands 'focus' – and that this focus must start with a selection process – refining the broad groups of potential customers into clearly defined segments. Only then can the technique of market research and sales forecasting be brought into play.

Market segmentation

The idea of market segmentation starts from the premise that, within a given market, there are different and, so far as possible, discrete groups of customers with different needs. Identifying these specific needs for these particular customers can be more profitable than simply 'scattering bread on the waters', or waiting for the 'passing trade' to come into the shop.

How does the product manager decide? If, for example, he has just arrived in a company which, whether in consumer goods or industrial products or services, has been 'around' for some time, the choice of market segment will be obvious. As a product manager in a tobacco company once said when asked what market segment his filter-tipped cigarette brand was aimed at, 'Those who smoke filter-tipped cigarettes'. Which, of course, was true but unhelpful. This demonstrates that the company is in the groove of its existing segmentation. You find when you take over as the new product manager ('with shining morning face!') that existing segmentation patterns are geographic (north, south, east, west, TV regions, population density, etc), demographic (age, income, socio-economic group, family size, etc) or purchase related (Ministry of Defence, steel-making industries, TV assemblers, etc). The theory being (if anyone has thought about the theoretical background) that such a segmentation is based on the marketing department's ability either to identify the segment, or to have access to it, via the appropriate promotion media.

After all, factories can be identified in directories, old people, poor people, posh people can be recognised on sight. And the readership of *The Times* or the cars passing Cromwell Road hoardings are accessible – if we want to sell to those people. The difficulty here is obvious. The people, buyers or potential customers who have been identified in this way do not necessarily share the same needs, nor seek the same benefits nor respond to the same messages.

The other approach which, as a new product manager, you may find is being used is based on customer needs. The products, you are informed, have been designed to 'deliver uniquely sought benefits to each significant market segment'. Of course this is the right way to do it. The needs/benefits approach has the advantage that this is ultimately the basis on which buyers make their decisions. So if we can discover the potential purchasers', buyers', users' needs and we can design products to fit them, we should have identified our market segments.

Two difficulties arise:

1. What might be called the 'Walkman' difficulty. This is the difficulty which interferes with the needs/benefit theory because it says 'No one needed a Walkman until the Walkman was produced'. To put it more formally 'buyer needs may only develop in interaction with new technologies which expand buyer opportunities in unexpected directions'.
2. The 'fortuitous overlap' difficulty (Figure 3.1). Buyers whom we can identify easily may (or may not) have the same needs and respond to the same benefits offered by the product or service.

Faced with this problem the product manager (new or experienced) has to identify more clearly the market segment or segments which he is aiming at. As a starting-point he can create a series of hypotheses which can then be translated into a matrix. Along the *horizontal* axis he should list the major identifiable or accessible characteristics of the potential purchasers of product or service. [Let us keep it simple at this stage and assume that the obvious characteristics are those of the purchaser. See p. 25 for a discussion of the problem of identifying the decision-making unit (DMU).] The *vertical* axis must show the motivations which are likely to be displayed towards the product or service offered.

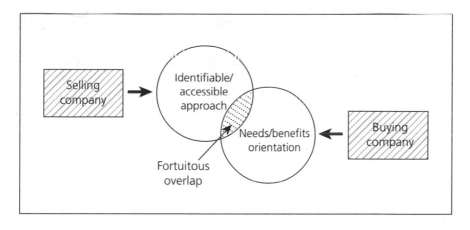

Figure 3.1 *Fortuitous overlap*

Three examples will serve to illustrate the process of constructing a matrix – a company which manufactures electronic components (see Figure 3.2), a firm selling industrial X-ray machines (Figure 3.3) and a large provincial hotel (Figure 3.4) which, although it did not have a product manager as such, had a conference manager, a marketing manager and a food and beverage manager – each of whom was responsible for one of the hotel's main products.

Electrical Components

		CHARACTERISTICS					
		TV Assembly	Radio HiFi	Industrial Controls	Other OEMs	Large Distributors	Small Distr
MOTIVATION	Quality						
	Reliability						
	Price						
	Flexibility						
	Innovation						

Figure 3.2 *Electronic components*

Industrial X-ray Machine

	CHARACTERISTICS				
	Pipeline Contractors	Commission Welders	Car Assembly	Consult. Engineers	Quality Assurance
Portability					
Reliability					
Cheap to run					
Easy to maintain					
Speed of decision					

(MOTIVATION — row label on left axis)

Figure 3.3 *Industrial X-ray machines*

Provincial Hotel

	CHARACTERISTICS				
	US Tourists	Dutch Tourists	Tour Operators	Radius 1½ hours train	Radius hours car
Sightseeing					
Relaxation					
Holiday					
Weekend break					
Discounts					
Status					
Golf					

(MOTIVATION — row label on left axis)

Figure 3.4 *Provincial hotel*

Having put together your matrix on the basis of knowledge, experience or hypothesis, the trick now is to identify the areas (boxes) which fit and which provide the largest actual or potential market. [In the first example it may seem likely that TV assembly customers are more interested in innovation or flexibility (samples quickly, small quantities for trials) than price. Distributors will probably be more interested in reliability (no problems) and price. In the second example, pipeline contractors will almost certainly be influenced by portability and reliability whereas car assemblers will require 'cheap to run' machines which offer 'speed of decision'. In the third example, the provincial hotel marketing manager will probably look for tour operators requiring discount or car owners within a radius of two hours' drive looking for a weekend break.]

In each case the matrix provides a logical starting-point for an excursion into market segments which can help the product managers to decide 'who to approach', 'what media to use' and 'what to say to them', 'what benefits to stress'. This will enable the product manager to focus activity on the segments with the most potential.

Two other points to make on the subject:

1. the matrix helps to indicate areas where market research is needed, that is, where the product manager needs more detailed information about either the demographics or the motivations of the segment;
2. the identification of the decision making unit (DMU) brings with it the need to create a matrix showing the different members of the DMU and their motivations (Figure 3.5).

		DMU MEMBERS				
		User	Influencer	Decision maker	Buyer	Gatekeeper
MOTIVATION	Ease of use					
	Price					
	Status of company					
	Previous history					

Figure 3.5 *Decision making unit*

EXAMPLE

The company produces 'background music' in the shape of four-hour tapes which it rents out to those who have purchased its 'players'. It originally considered it was in the 'selling of background music tape players'. It discovered that in one market 'commission agents' were asking for specific types of music to offer to different markets. The marketing plan was revamped to fit markets as shown in Table 3.1.

Table 3.1 *Revamped market fit*

Outlet	Player type	Music type	Motivation
Hotel	Four-hour repeat	Classic/light classic	Ambience
Restaurant	Four-hour repeat	Light orchestral	Privacy
Bar/cafe	Four-hour repeat	Jazz/rock/pop	Feel at home
Doctor's waiting room	Four-hour repeat	Light/gentle	Reassurance
Dentist's surgery	Four-hour repeat	Relaxation	Distraction
Jewellery shop	Four-hour repeat and message	Light modern	Ambience Status
Department store	Two-hour repeat with message	Modern	Ambience Status
Supermarket	Two-hour repeat with message	Upbeat	Encourage to stay

So that in any geographical district the actual numbers of outlets could be identified, the forecast of expected sales of players and the hire of tapes was more accurate, the 'mood' of the tapes could be established and numbers derived. This gave the 'mood engineer' an indication of what sort of music he should search out and record on the different tapes offered.

DMU theory

Every decision to purchase a product or service is influenced by one or more members of the so-called decision-making unit (DMU). Broadly, this comprises:

- *The user* – the person who will use the product or service.
- *The influencer* – usually someone whose advice is requested or offered which as a result can influence the brand, the manufacturer, price, timing, etc, of the purchase.
- *The decision maker* – the ultimate maker of the decision to purchase the service or product (remember that it can be a committee).
- *The buyer* – the purchasing officer who has responsibility for the purchasing budget and therefore of getting the best value for money.
- *The gatekeeper* – literally he or she who controls access to the rest of the decision-making unit: perhaps an information provider, a secretary or a security manager.

The theory comes into play when the members of the DMU are identified and their motivations are assessed.

RESEARCHING THE SEGMENT

Market research is concerned with trying to quantify results and to assess the reasons for those results. Quantification is the adding up of numbers of outlets, sales per outlet and ranking outlets and the assessment of likely future sales.

The development of market research over the years has ensured that a great deal of research has been produced so that there are a number of professional agencies which can provide all the technical aspects of market research. Apart from a satisfactory brief to a market research agency there are three questions a product manager *must* ask.

The first is: 'What will we do with the information when we've got it?' Many research reports get consigned either to the shredder ('We know all that anyway; we've known it for years. We don't need another report!') or to the desk drawer ('Don't agree with that! Common sense tells me that's rubbish! Clearly they've asked the wrong questions.'). It is important, therefore, to decide *before* undertaking market research of whatever shape or size, what will be done with the conclusions and recommendations which arise from it. In political polling, 51 per cent is a majority and the views of the minority become totally unimportant. In commercial market research the proportion, size, numbers, locations and views of the whole market are important and can influence strategy.

The second question to ask is: 'How far will the information be reliable?' In these days much of the original argument about whether a 'sample' was truly representative of the universe has been left behind. Statistical methods have proved the reliability of sampling as indicative of the views of the 'universe' to within known and calculated margins of error. Worries about reliability are centred on three problems:

1. *Memory*. We are not good at remembering unimportant events and actions – things like purchases made, reasons for decisions, advertisements seen, product names, etc. As a result when asked by a market researcher in front of us or on the telephone or when faced with a questionnaire, our 'remembrance of things past' tends to be unreliable. (Witnesses to events which have occurred only minutes earlier will disagree about fundamentals like colour, size or shape.)
2. *Understanding*. It is very difficult to get a reliable answer if the respondent does not understand the question [try creating a question about a current political situation and see if anyone understands it!] or if the respondent's background and therefore assumptions and starting points are different from those of the questioner.
3. *The respondent's view of himself*. There is a wide spectrum of questions which can be asked of people and which are liable to get an unreliable answer; they are the questions where the answer threatens the respondent's own pride. We all fear personal questions. [Try asking a group of people how much they drink. The answers will range from 'ten pints a night' to 'an occasional small sherry'. The truth of these answers will be very dubious.] This problem can often be made worse by the (apparent) social difference between questioner and respondent.

Clearly it is vital to ensure that the answers to the questions do not depend for their reliability on faulty memory, high IQ or sensitive respondents.

The third question is: 'How much will it cost?' Again the answer to this question is not simple. The cost can be defined simply as the fee requested by the agency – and it can be seen as the choice of agency, ranging from a large well-known London-based market research agency, a small provincial firm, the local business school students looking for a project, to the local school sixth form whose mathematics teacher understands statistics and is keen to introduce his pupils to the 'real' world. Cost can also be defined as the cost of not taking decisions which the research shows ought to be taken or taking decisions which go against a survey's findings.

The answers to all three questions need to be established clearly *before* the research goes ahead, so that a full brief can be given to the agency which is carrying out the research.

COLLECTING INFORMATION

Much information both for consumer and industrial market segments may be available already in published sources, government publications, trade publications, private research (Mintel, Economist Intelligence Unit, etc). Public libraries are a good source. Once this has been trawled one can then attempt further investigation. This 'desk research' can often act as the basis for 'field research'; this in turn can be undertaken by:

Method	Plus point	Disadvantage
Postal questionnaire	Cheapness	Self-selected sample
Telemarket research	Focused	Limited questions
Face-to-face	Accurate sample	Expensive

(Additionally, it is often suggested that some kind of incentive should be offered for returning the questionnaire. This quite often increases the response rate of a postal questionnaire but may not produce any more 'reliable' answers.)

Where a small and focused market (groups of potential customers) has been identified, it has been found that telephoning the respondent first and *then* sending a questionnaire can improve the response rate dramatically.

Frequently a major problem for businesses concerned with both product and service is not knowing why the product or service is *not* purchased. In consumer products a great deal of information is produced through sales invoices, Nielsen reports of outlet sales, etc. When sales go down it is often very difficult to understand the reason (and we go on hoping things will get better, until it is too late to make a dramatic improvement). One answer is the 'focus group' – currently popular with political parties – which comprises a free ranging discussion among a group (about 20) of potential and actual purchasers/users on the merits and weaknesses of the product or service. Such a discussion can very often uncover serious defects in the 'image', presentation, packaging, advertising and after-sales service of a product. The driving force in recommending the use of such a focus group would be the product manager!

USING INFORMATION

Cyril Anson, a guru in the application of statistics to management decisions, remarks: 'Forecasting reinforces managerial judgement; it is not a substitute for it'. The product manager's function is to bring together the information which will provide 'an estimate of the quantitative and qualitative characteristics of the future developments in the market in which an organisation operates' (Anson).

Here is a step-by-step approach for the product manager on how to create a forecast:

1. *Analyse past sales.* Since what may happen next year is likely to be to a greater extent a repeat of what happened last year, it is essential to examine trends and actual figures of sales over the past five years or so [eg a clothes manufacturer regularly sells 85 per cent of his range in classic styles, year after year – even though bringing out a new and dramatic 'collection' each year].
2. *Eliminate seasonality.* In a business which has strong seasonal fluctuations (summer, winter, biannual ordering, holiday periods) it is valuable to assess figures on a moving annual total (MAT) basis or expressing sales figures as a percentage of the average sales for the period
   [eg   Annual sales   12 million
          Average sales   1 million per month
          This month sales   970,000 = 97 per cent
          Last month sales   450,000 = 45 per cent.]
3. *Project trends.* Taking the existing sales (for the last four years) it is now possible to project trends into the future, next year, month by month, quarter by quarter, on your PC, by:
   - straight line projections;
   - least squares projection;
   - exponential smoothing.

All these programmes are available in the software package of most PCs. These programmes should be checked for obvious errors.

4. *Assess the likely effects of changes (internal).* A very difficult part of any sales forecast, unless the product manager has knowledge of the effects of past changes in:
   - types of product, or new ranges;
   - special advertising activities;
   - expansion of outlets or markets;
   - changes in channels or prices;
   - increase or decrease in salesforce.

5. *Assess likely effects of changes (external).* This refers to dramatic changes, expected or known, in the activities or products of major competitors (this may require market research to uncover).

6. *Allow for external changes in the market:*
   - demographic changes (very slow);
   - income changes (difficult to predict);
   - climatic changes (English weather);
   - government's fiscal and taxation policies.

7. *Check* against the views of those for whom the forecast is an essential tool for their planning. Unless the product manager obtains a consensus, then each of the operational departments will make its own assumptions and produce its own internal forecast.

Using Moving Annual Totals (MAT) helps to give an overall view of sales figures, output figures, consumption figures etc which by ironing out seasonal fluctuations helps to present a balanced view of the past and therefore can provide a more realistic pattern of the future. The data provided in this form are rarely available from accounts departments, since they are usually constrained by the financial year.

Creation of an MAT cannot start until Year 2, as can be seen from the following table; the monthly figures for Year 1 are the basic raw material.

Starting in the first month of Year 2 (say 31st January) the monthly sales of January Year 2 are added to the cumulative total of Year 1 and the sales of January Year 1 are subtracted (386 + 12 - 10 = 388) and so on, month by month. The MAT is then plotted on the graph and tends to reveal real changes in demand.

In order to create a 'Z' chart, monthly sales are plotted along the bottom of the graph, cumulative sales as a rising curve, with the MAT at the top. The advantage of this simple control is that most

Table 3.1

Month	Sales Year 1	Sales Year 2	Euros € '000s MAT in Year 2	Sales Year 3	MAT in Year 3
Jan	10	12	388	13	393
Feb	15	14	387	16	395
Mar	30	28	385	30	397
Apr	32	35	388	31	393
May	34	37	391	38	394
Jun	38	42	395	40	392
July	40	40	395	42	394
Aug	31	27	391	29	396
Sep	40	38	389	40	398
Oct	38	35	386	39	402
Nov	36	39	389	41	404
Dec	42	45	392	43	402
Cum Total	386	392		402	

of the vital information can be expressed in comparative form on one easily understood graph. It can diminish attempts at panic action. Target or budget lines can also be imposed on the graph in advance, to provide reference points throughout the year.

The basic information on which to construct the forecast can come from the following sources, all of whose input is important:

■ Salesforce expectations of sales volume and value.*
■ Salesforce reports on users' expectations.*
■ Statistical approaches: trend lines, least squares, exponential smoothing, probabilities.
■ Information about indicators.[†]
■ Views of independent experienced 'jury'.

---

* To try to make salesforce judgements more realistic, it is often worthwhile to ask them to make three estimates: optimistic (O), pessimistic (P) and most likely (ML). Product managers can then use the formula:

$$\frac{O + 4 \times ML + P}{6} = \text{Best Forecast.}$$

[†]Development of indicators is often useful when involved in joint (eg components in a machine or product, accessories for a product) or separate events which may impinge on the organisation's results (eg currency devaluations on tourism).

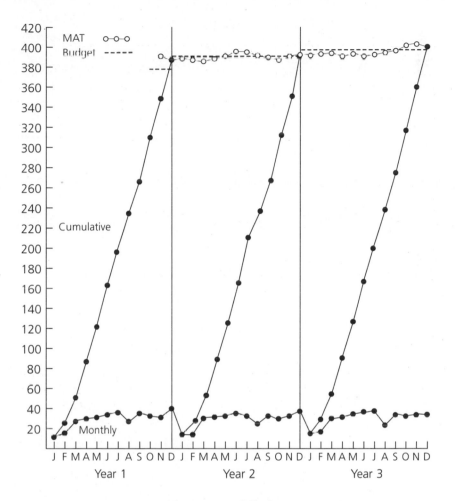

Figure 3.6 *'Z' chart*

CHECKLIST

- Have you a standard outline of a product plan?
- On what basis do you segment your market?
- Do you have ongoing market research to validate your assumptions?
- Is a sales forecast made?
- Does it contain monthly estimates of both volume and value?
- Is it discussed with production planners, sales managers and promotion/communication departments?

4

Developing the Product Plan: The Product

As shown in Chapter 3, the second part of the product plan involves a careful look at the product. If the product manager is to manage her product then she has to understand not only the process of manufacture from A–Z but also the process of consumption by the consumer (client, purchaser, user).

This chapter covers the steps to be taken by the product manager (for the sake of argument, she is newly appointed).

1. Look inwards, evaluate the existing product range.
2. Look at the way competitors help customers to solve the same problems.
3. Assess the ways in which consumers think and behave.
4. Examine the strategic analysis techniques which have been developed over the past decade or so to help managers make decisions about products.

EVALUATING THE RANGE OR THE LINE

Few product managers are responsible for a sole product. They are generally given responsibility for a range of products, which can be variants of the same 'problem solver' *or* related by manufacturing methods, (eg a range of different coloured and embossed PVC sheets); *or* by distribution methods, (eg a range of electronics components all of which may be handled by the same distributor); *or* by similar consumption systems, (eg televisions and videos, washing powder and softener, advertising and sales promotion services).

It is therefore very worthwhile either to use a standard checklist or to create your own. [*Note:* a checklist is intended to ensure that the right questions are asked. It does not, nor should it, provide the answers. Many managers (product managers among them) think that once a checklist has been created the job is done; all the answers have been found – a dangerous assumption!] Such a checklist should cover, at least, the following areas (there is no order of importance as this will vary depending on type of product or service).

Scope of the product line

In many organisations there is a kind of pendulum effect. Product managers (or marketing managers) are either trying to cut out unprofitable products to reduce the size of the range or trying to broaden the scope of the range in order to meet competitive challenges. The pressure to reduce the number of products comes from:

1. increases caused by production costs incurred with more product varieties;
2. increased space and handling costs in warehouses due to stock holding; and
3. the difficulties of the salesforce having to cope with a greater variety of products and the need to give each product its due quantity of selling effort.

In many businesses too many products are launched for fear of the dangers of specialisation and the thought that diversification invariably adds to market strength. Nowadays, however, many sprawling multi-businesses are trying desperately to cut back to what is called their 'core' business and in the process they are rationalising their product ranges, selling off parts of the business and trying to concentrate on the most profitable areas of the business. Balancing that is the pendulum swing the other way. There are pressures to produce new and improved products. Pressures come from:

1. competitors, who always seem to be producing something which can nibble away at our market;
2. our standing in the market which 'demands' that we cover the whole range of customer requirements;
3. our 'image' as a producer which means that we need to provide for every smallest niche market;
4. the sales department, which being in the 'blood and sawdust ring', feels that the only way to fight is to match competitors' products exactly.

Marketing efficiency

Costs seem to increase all the time. Those under the control of marketing need to be monitored carefully – particularly those of physical handling, packing, storing and delivery of increasing numbers of products.

Check the following:

■ Do you know the real allocated costs of marketing each product or service and of the necessary variants and 'specials'?
■ What level of contribution are these products giving? (Not on average but in actuality!)
■ Is the market niche big enough to support the costs of marketing the products?
■ Is the contribution adequate to cover the (objectively) right marketing mix? (See Chapters 7 and 11.)

Production costs and quality

Areas of production should be looked at by the product manager (she will have to be doubly tactful, as production executives are usually even more sensitive to criticism than sales managers!)

Start with quality. (It is interesting to note that service quality is usually judged on the basis of the customer's reaction (for example a KLM advertisement: 'Service quality is not the smile on the face of the stewardess, but the smile on the face of the customer').) The quality of a product is often judged on whether it is manufactured to the required specification, defects are within tolerable limits, etc. The current basic quality standard of BS5750 (ISO 9000) is merely a guarantee that the product has been produced along established lines and procedures. (Total quality management (TQM) however, taking BS5750 as a base, moves much further in the direction of fitting the product to the customer.)

The first question is whether methods of manufacture have been examined (using such techniques as value analysis, method study, production engineering and, for services, activity sampling) so as to ensure maximum productivity with no loss of customer satisfaction. [*Note:* the product manager has to engineer measurement of customer satisfaction through qualitative market research – see Chapter 3.]

The second question is what do you do if the product is simply a 'given' – for example an airline route, a standard capacitor or a porcelain shape? The product manager needs to question whether the product can be disguised, repackaged, sold as part of something else, changed in the perception of the customer. [A useful exercise for a product manager is to find examples within her own experience of this being done, eg Kellogg's Corn Flakes for eating in the evening, an airline route being sold as part of a larger holiday package.]

What are the costs of variety? With the development of computer controlled manufacturing processes the ability of the production system to produce infinite variety is now a fact. Even in service provision – a hotel as a conference centre, a coach as a package tour instrument, a building society as a bank – there are many examples of organisations either embracing variety regardless of cost or of *not* risking variety because of a false expectation of high cost.

Price and value

The product manager needs to examine the prices of her products under four headings:

1. *Competition* – asking the question 'Is the product, from the point of view of the customer or client, roughly in line with that of my competitor?'
2. *Market slot* – does the product fit within an accepted slot in the market or is it completely out of line? [Checks need to be carried out in the marketplace to gauge the size of the price slot.]
3. *Distributors' margins* – are the products priced in such a way as to provide the distributor (wholesaler, retailer or agent) with a margin which will satisfy him/her?
4. *Pricing strategy* – is there a pricing strategy which takes account of market requirements? (See Chapter 6 for a discussion of pricing strategies.)

As for *value*, it was Adam Smith who first expounded the difference between 'value in use' and 'value in esteem'. The product manager's task is to try to measure the difference between the functional efficiency of the product and whatever it is (appearance, brand, status enhancement) which creates a desire to possess the product or use the service. The salesforce should have a good idea what the 'X' factor is, that is the factor which enhances the value beyond the value in use. [For example, travelling first class on an airline does not get you to your destination any more quickly than travelling economy or business class. However, there are still a number of passengers who prefer to pay the much higher fare. On the other hand there is a school of thought which asserts that 'First Class' is a different product!]

Service

Over the past few years the concept of service has become concentrated more on maintaining customer satisfaction with the product as it is than on repair and maintenance of the product itself (this is most evident in the automobile market). Thus it becomes necessary to teach principles of service to the service providers and to cost the provision of that extra service into the basic costs of the product. (With a service you cannot just expect the client to 'throw it away and purchase another one'.) Many products and product accessories are now created with 'replacement' rather than 'repairable' sections because the balance in many cases is on the cost of replacement rather than repair.

Nevertheless the product manager needs carefully to evaluate the costs and benefits of servicing her product. The valuation can be transferred to a checksheet like the one in Table 4.1.

COMPETITIVE APPRAISAL

Comparison with what competitors are offering is always difficult. Product managers are confronted usually with two (or more) opposing views. The production engineer (or R&D or operator) will almost always prove that the competitor's product is inferior to the product which her company produces. The sales manager and salesmen will demonstrate that the competitive product is not only superior but also cheaper.

Table 4.1 *Evaluating the range*

Subject	Examined	Result	Action	Control date
Scope of the line	July 1997	Increase/ decrease	ABC departments	September
Marketing efficiency	Discuss with sales	Reallocate costs	Marketing Information Systems	December
Production costs and quality	Production and accounts	R & D?	Development committee	30 June
Price and value	Sales force research	Report submitted	Sales manager	January
Service	Quality training	Programme created	Administration staff	Ongoing

To try to combat such subjective views it is recommended that the product manager creates a table such as Table 4.2, and requests both factions to fill in both the aspects of relative importance and the strengths and weaknesses of competitive offerings. Only when this is done can any positive recommendations be made as to what improvements can be undertaken.

Table 4.2 was constructed around a large and expensive capital good. The principles however remain the same:

■ first list the marketing factors which affect the customer, client, user, etc – usually under some main headings;
■ then establish which factors play an important part in the customer's choice;
■ then assess the strength or weakness both of your own organisation and that of two or three major competitors.

This can be done for large capital goods, for small accessories or components, for packaged products or for different kinds of services (mass market services such as banks, professional services such as lawyers or capital intensive services such as hotels or airlines).

Table 4.2 *Competitive appraisal of the products*

		Competitive Appraisal – Strengths and Weaknesses Product		
Relative Importance	Marketing Factors	ABC Ltd Weak/Strong 1, 2, 3, 4, 5	Competitor Weak/Strong 1, 2, 3, 4, 5	Competitor Weak/Strong 1, 2, 3, 4, 5
	PRODUCT Fitness for Purpose			
	Technology: Life Span			
	Update			
	Output Quality			
	Reliability			
	Total Package			
	Design & Appearance			
	PRICE Selling Price			
	Credit Terms			
	Operating Costs			
	Cost of Ownership			
	Maintenance Costs			
	PROMOTION EFFECTIVENESS Advertising			
	Company Image			
	Exhibitions			
	Commercial Demonstr.			
	SALESMANSHIP Product Knowledge			
	Call Regularity			
	Problem Solving			
	DISTRIBUTION Ease of Ordering			
	Availability			
	Delivery Performance			
	SERVICE Sales Administration			
	Installation			
	After Sales Service			
	Warranty			
	Training			
	Service Manuals			

EXAMPLE: DECIDING ON THE RANGE OF PRODUCTS FOR THE GARAGE FORECOURT SHOP

'What's marketing about, then?' he replied, after I had asked him whether he made use of marketing techniques in his business.

'It's a sort of philosophy,' I explained, 'but it comes in very handy when you want to improve your business performance.'

'But,' he said, 'I'm just a wholesaler to garage forecourt shops, why would I need marketing? Isn't that just for the big boys like Esso and Shell?'

'Well . . . for a start, who are your customers? Presumably the managers of garages.'

'Uh . . . yes,' he answered, 'but I think they're probably the people in cars who buy the things I supply.'

'Have you,' I continued, 'ever done any market research?'

'You mean ask lots of questions of people who're already in a hurry? Not likely!'

'Well, how do you know what they want?'

'I just go round and talk to my customers and their staff.'

'And what do they tell you?' I probed.

'Well, they say that people who buy stuff in forecourt shops do so for four or five reasons.'

'Which are?'

'There's the chap who's forgotten to get batteries for his Walkman, or a film for his camera or milk or bread, or occasionally, someone who needs a map.'

'Emergency purchases, perhaps?' I said.

'You could say that, but there's a lot of food sold nowadays – and I don't touch food. Too much waste! But there's also the dad whose greatest need is to keep the kids quiet, so he buys toys or sweets.'

'How many of them are there, do you think?'

'Quite a few, but not as many as the ones who've forgotten to get something for the wife, partner or girlfriend. They're late or something. So they buy a box of chocolates, bunch of flowers or – we do a good trade in silk underwear! Guilt purchases, I suppose. Increasing all the time!'

'And . . . what else?'

'There's all the stuff we sell which can only be taken home in the boot: barbecue fuel, garden furniture and logs mostly. And the little extra things for men only: expensive models of cars, top shelf mags and the like . . .'

'So that's how you decide on your product range, is it? And how do you decide on the price?'

'Well, there's not a lot of competition. No one's going to look at the goods and say, "Perhaps I'll get it cheaper down the road." So we price to make a fair profit. I always say the price must be acceptable to the customer, give a margin to the garage, and provide me with a profit. So we don't insult customers with silly prices like £1.99 when a perfectly accept-able price would be £2.15!'

'So,' I said, 'you do actually carry out marketing. You research your customers' requirements, segment your market, provide products to fit, price them acceptably and check regularly the effectiveness of your sales patterns and shop layouts.'

'Really!' he said. 'So I've been doing marketing all along. Is that good?'

'Great!' I replied. 'Now all you need is to improve your ordering and distribution systems . . .' Needless to add, I suggested he get some help with that.

PURCHASE AND CONSUMPTION BEHAVIOUR

The product manager (more than anyone else) needs to understand how consumers are likely to respond to marketing stimuli.

Consumer buying behaviour

Much research, often taken over from academic psychiatrists and psychologists, has gone into the attempt to understand how buyers' minds work. Models have been created in order to assess the rationality or irrationality of behaviour. Most researchers agree that consumers are influenced by cultural, social, personal and psychological characteristics. (For a more complete discussion see O'Shaughnessy, 1987).

Cultural factors include learned values and ways of doing things, which may stem from nationality or tradition, geography or socio-economic grouping. The generally accepted social groupings in the UK, originally set up by the National Readership Survey, are as follows:

Grade	Social status	Head of household
A	Upper middle class	Higher managerial, administrative or professional

B	Middle class	Intermediate managerial, administrative or professional
C1	Lower middle class	Supervisory or clerical and junior managerial, administrative or professional
C2	Skilled working class	Skilled manual workers
D	Working class	Semi-skilled and unskilled manual workers
E	Those at lowest levels of subsistence	State pensioners, widows, casual or lowest grade workers

Social factors include the reference groups to which consumers belong both formally and informally (and perhaps also to which they aspire), family (both older and younger generation) and the role the consumer plays in each group – wife, daughter, brand manager, local youth leader, etc. [Additionally there has been developed in the UK a concept called ACORN (Classification of Residential Neighbourhoods) based on census information about the areas where people live which splits the whole population into 39 classifications.]

Personal factors include, most obviously, age and life-cycle stage (largely affected by arrival, upbringing and departure of children), occupation and economic circumstances; less obviously in terms of lifestyle, expressed as a pattern of living (more particularly Stanford Research Institute's concept of Values and Life Styles, VALS).

Psychological factors include motivation, perception, learning and beliefs, each of which affects the purchase decision to a greater or lesser degree. Individuals are motivated by needs, and once a need is uncovered the individual tends to select a 'goal' which will satisfy that need – provided, that is, the appropriate product or service exists. (Until a fast ferry was put into service to travel from Harwich to the Hook of Holland, a grandmother's need to cross the North Sea in less than seven hours at a reasonable price to give presents to her grandchildren could not be satisfied.)

Understanding motivations can help both advertising and sales people to provide the right kind of stimulus needed to produce a favourable response. The 'trigger' can be found:

■ in the *shape* of an article – the Ford *Ka*, even though a tiny vehicle, is designed so that the shape appeals to the 'devil-may-care' young;

- in the *colour* – it has been suggested that colouring DIY tools purple will motivate more women to purchase them;
- in the *distribution pattern* - items on the top shelves of super-markets are for tall people, while goods stocked by Harrods are aimed at the rich;
- in the *description or the advertising slogan* - such as Peugeot's 'the drive of your life' or BMW's 'the ultimate driving machine'.

The success of such 'triggers' will depend on how the potential purchaser perceives it, rather than how the 'creator' sees it. For example, it is said that the British machine-tool industry died because it took the view that machine-tools should be strong, heavy and grey, and designed to last a long time. In contrast, German and Italian machine-tools arrived in the UK, made of more interesting materials, lighter in weight and painted in lively colours. These foreign tools made the toolshop seem a more exciting place to work in the eyes of the 'users' and eventually they took over much of the market. The Japanese then followed the German lead!

Speed of learning is also a factor in the acceptability level of the product. For example, it is a well-known phenomenon that children assimilate to computers more quickly and easily than adults. Children *learn* faster than adults and with less stress, particularly when there is, for them, a satisfying result to be gained from the learning.

Attitudes have a bearing on the willingness or unwillingness to accept messages (advertisements, sales promotion and packaging) about a product. This is a particular problem with innovative products or changed products. A natural suspicion of the 'new', and cynicism about much advertising, seems to affect purchasers. Attitudes and behaviour are also, very often, derived from the group, the gang, the social set or the fan club to which the purchaser belongs. Weight may be given to *'what my friends and acquaintances may think'*. Bearing these aspects in mind, a brand or corporate image can be developed after careful research by product managers *(see Chapter 9)*.

Buyer behaviour patterns (or models) need to be established for products or services so that marketing activities can be aimed at the point where the maximum impact will be made.

Industrial buying behaviour

It is often thought that because industrial purchasers are professional they are in some way insulated from normal human feelings and do not behave like consumers. This is evidently not true but there are additional considerations to be taken into account when trying to influence 'industrial', 'professional', or 'capital goods' purchasers.

In particular, two ideas have been explored much in recent years – the decision-making unit and the buying situation. Indeed, attempts have been made to put them together. The decision-making unit (DMU) can consist of any or all of the following:

■ the user;
■ the decision maker;
■ the influencer;
■ the buyer;
■ the gatekeeper (see Chapter 3).

Each one's approach to the purchase (of goods or services) probably will be different. At an early stage in any marketing approach it is therefore necessary to identify to whom the message is to be directed (by mail, phone, advertisement, sales call, etc) and who the members of the DMU might be. In the case of government or local authority purchasing a committee might well contain all of these functions.

The buying situations, which also need to be planned for, are as follows:

■ straight rebuy, where the purchaser simply reorders without modification, a routine operation;
■ modified rebuy, where a purchaser desires to change the specification or price or terms, or seeks a second source;
■ new purchase, where a producer or system or service is being purchased for the first time and the purchaser is seeking to minimise her risk in a situation where she feels in greatest uncertainty.

The aspects of risk and risk perception are a third area where industrial purchase decisions have been researched. Risks which the buyer tries to avoid are:

■ wrong specification;
■ relationship to production process (mismatch);
■ competitive offers (better and cheaper);
■ technology changes (before commitment);
■ delivery dates (too late);
■ price levels (too high);
■ standards of vendor.

Marketing activities of vendors need to be adapted to the reduction of risk and uncertainty.

Customer perception

The product manager also is vitally interested in how the customer sees the product or service; and in the collection of three kinds of information about her product – strategic, usage and competitive. Strategic information should help to answer the questions as to what future the product has or should have. Usage information concerns the way in which the customer currently uses the product, its importance to the user and what problems it solves. Competitive information should cover not only directly competitive products but also competitive ways of solving the problem. What does the customer do if neither our product nor that of our competitors is being used (eg 'Do-it-yourself' conveyancing, *not* going on a package tour)?

Strategic questions are those such as: 'Where does the product fit in the customer's consumption system?' This can be either a literal system, such as the way a person does the weekly wash, or a model of how a potential customer deals with the problem of spending or saving money. It can have a literal strength in establishing the size of the container (a bottle, a carton, a refrigerator) or it can have a philosophical importance in establishing the point at which a customer makes a decision to use a certain service (her social perception of it, changes in social and ethical valuation, etc). Information is sought to answer strategic questions such as: 'What should be the thrust of our product policy in the next five years?' A second and perhaps more important strategic question is: 'Will the product retain its importance for the current buyers in the next few years?' Alternatively, will some new product make the present method obsolete, or some service ('pizzas at home') solve an existing problem?

Usage information results from questions such as: 'How does the customer use the product or service?' Often the inventors or distributors of a product or service find that the users are 'contrary' individuals who find ways of using it which are not what they originally intended. Human ingenuity, impatience or perhaps 'bloody-mindedness' create a gap between the product designer and the user which has to be bridged by information. Too often this bridge is not achieved and it is assumed that the service or product is used in a certain way which in the majority of cases is far from the norm. Such information is often called 'customer information' and can be the most difficult to collect because many people are unable or unwilling to explain exactly how they use a product. Often the way to discover it is to observe the product or service in use.

Competitive information starts with information which ranks competitors in order of importance either by their image or their market share. Some assessment ought then to be made of their strategy – how they see the market and what their strengths and weaknesses are (in products, prices, development, channels of distribution and methods of after-sales service). There are, of course, dangers in collecting information about competitors' approaches to customers: policy can be directed too much towards meeting competition and too little towards meeting customer requirements. One can be altogether too busy worrying about the competitor's next move to see major changes in the environment. Nevertheless, an awareness of relative market share and competitors' main strengths and weaknesses is an essential basis for evaluating one's own products (see Table 4.2, Page 40).

Differential advantage

The product manager also needs to establish the 'differential advantage' of her product or service. If it has one, what is it? If it does not, what could it be? In the past this aspect may have been called a unique selling proposition (USP) but a differential advantage has far wider implications. So the product manager should look at:

1. *Specific features* – something which her product possesses and others do not which allows it to be demonstrably different (Audi developed a five-cylinder engine, Little Chef have a standard menu, Saga understand the over 50s). The feature must be something which the client recognises. Too often features are added which simply confuse customers, providing possibilities which the customer rarely, if ever, needs (eg video remote control 'zappers').

2. *Image* – very often a differential advantage can arise based simply on the image of an organisation, a product or a service. [A customer constantly complained that electronic components purchased from supplier M were 10 per cent more expensive than those from suppliers R and S. His purchases, however, were divided equally across all three suppliers because M's reputation for helping out and going to great trouble and expense was unique in that trade.] The image can result from experience of

customers and their recognition of the status of the organisation (Harrods' plastic bags are treasured!) or from the reliability and consistent quality given by the organisation.

3. *Fitness for purpose* – examples abound of products and services which are not fit for their purpose or at least not quite good enough. The product manager needs to establish with all concerned – from creator to consumer – precisely what the purpose is and only then look at the fitness of her product or service for that purpose. Success carries a considerable reward (examine the success of the Land Rover, look at the suitability of wine boxes, marvel at the Amstrad word-processor!).

4. *Price* – it is often said that the customer considers price to be an indication of quality. This is clearly partly true in areas where the customer has insufficient knowledge or information to assess the specification. [Is an expensive meal better than a cheap one?] The use of price as a differential advantage is better considered as value for money and since value is often a subjective aspect, it is very difficult to compare competitive offerings.

STRATEGIC CHOICE

The product manager is also the person who should identify the strategy to be followed for the marketing of her product (or perhaps the strategy currently being followed, if any). Various strategies have been identified in the literature, some of which are now out of date, and some which require more careful analysis.

An *undifferentiated* strategy is one which treats the market as totally homogeneous, ignores all differences and assumes that the same product has the same appeal to everyone, whether at home or abroad (sometimes called 'global marketing'). [Classic examples might be Coca-Cola, Gillette razors, McDonald's.] Promotional activities, channels of distribution, packaging and communications can be standardised. The great majority of products, however, cannot be treated this way.

A *differentiated* strategy is more common. Each market segment (see Chapter 3) is deemed to require a different product and a different marketing programme – perhaps a semi-custom-built product for each segment. This is most evident in products where there is a considerable amount of export business or perhaps in the motor car industry, where each segment demands a slightly different approach in terms of colour, trim, accessories and the like, for what is essentially a standard product. Airlines have come under much criticism in recent years for having been forced into a situation where they are producing what is essentially the same product, (ie transport between two points) and selling it to different groups of passengers: businessmen, tourists, families visiting relatives, etc. They try to make the product look different, they charge different prices for it but in essence it is the same product. However, the marketing of the product is totally different for each segment; for example, for businessmen the marketing takes place by means of contact through travel agents and travel managers; tickets are bought, seats are reserved; there is a possibility of changing the reservation; there is a possibility of cancelling the flight altogether without penalty. A holiday maker, on the other hand, usually buys a ticket as part of a package sold to him or her via a tour operator and through a travel agent. He/she often has to buy it well in advance, paying a deposit to show good intentions, and if he/she changes or cancels the original agreement then he/she pays a penalty for this privilege. However, the holiday maker also gets the ticket for the transport between two points at about half the price the businessperson pays for similar transport. To encourage the businessperson to believe that he/she is getting better value for money, all airlines have now developed an improved product called 'business class'.

A *niche* strategy develops from the idea behind the 'business class' product. A specific market segment is identified and the company goes after its share of that segment – by specialising the product or service, focusing the communication strategy, picking special distribution channels and pricing the product/service to fit the segment.

STRATEGIC ANALYSIS

In recent years two analytical techniques have become popular, both suggesting strategies which can be undertaken.

Cash flow strategies or product portfolio analysis

This technique is based on the production of a quadrant which sets off market share against market growth. (Historically the need for this analysis arose from the difficulty of deciding which product group to support and which to 'rule out!'.)

The importance of market share as a measurement tool was highlighted by research done by the Boston Consulting Group with the phenomenon of the 'experience curve'. It is obvious that the more times you do something the better you get at it (practising the piano, for example). Research showed that there was a relationship between cumulative output and the real costs of production.

An experience curve is plotted with the cumulative units produced on the horizontal axis and cost per unit on the vertical axis. An '85 per cent' experience curve is shown in Figure 4.1. The '85 per cent' means that every time experience doubles, costs per unit drop to 85 per cent of the original level. This is known as the *learning rate*. Stated differently, costs per unit decrease 15 per cent for every doubling of cumulative production, i.e. the cost of the 20th unit is about 85 per cent of the cost of the tenth unit. (This effect was seen in products and services as varied as steam turbine generators and long distance telephone rates.)

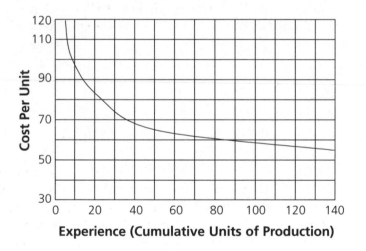

Figure 4.1 *Experience curve*

Source: *Abell and Hammond, Strategic Market Planning*

The importance of the experience curve lies in its relationship to market share. Postulate a large share of the market and the chances are that the company/organisation with that share will have lower real costs than a competitor with a smaller market share. (Of course, there are exceptions but in general this is likely to be the case when competitors have widely varying market share and similar products.)

The other axis in the quadrant is an estimate (or precise statistic) of the product's market growth rate (this will also be demonstrated in the product's life cycle – see Chapter 8) because both these axes will affect the rate at which cash is generated and therefore will provide some indication of the major strategies to be followed. The normal diagram which demonstrates the product portfolio analysis is as shown in Figure 4.2.

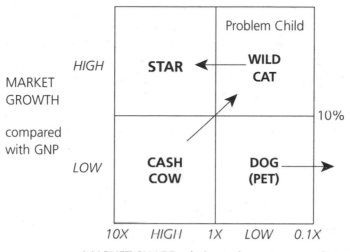

Figure 4.2 *Product portfolio quadrant*

Abell and Hammond show that the horizontal axis demonstrates 'cash generation' and the vertical axis shows 'cash use'. Other writers have drawn conclusions as to the appropriate course of action resulting from the analysis. The quadrant shows market share as relative to your largest competitor and market growth relative to GNP growth (always assuming that GNP is growing!).

Choosing a strategy

Once the product manager has positioned her product in the quadrant certain approaches to strategy become mandatory:

1. If you are the product manager of a *Cash Cow* (low growth, dominant market share) which generates more cash than is required to maintain that share, then your strategies should include recognition that:

- increase in market share can only be at the expense of competitors' capacity;
- maintenance of share requires pricing leadership and resistance to proliferation;
- cash generated may be more useful applied to R&D or to the support of products in growing markets.

2. If you are in charge of a *Star* (high growth and a dominant market share) then your strategies must recognise:
   - the need for cash to finance the rate of growth;
   - the direction of strategy towards an increased share of new users by reinvesting earnings in the form of price reductions, product improvement, better market coverage or production efficiency.

3. It is an unfortunate fact that the greatest number of products must be categorised as *Dogs* (low growth and low market share relative to the largest competitor). So there will be many product managers who must manage 'Dogs'. Most markets do not show signs of growth and market share gains will be fought over fiercely. A number of possible strategies present themselves (varying from 'despair' to 'hope'):
   - *closing* the product down, giving up the service;
   - *divestment* by the company, perhaps selling the whole product line as a going concern to a competitor to make a viable business;
   - *harvesting* by cutting back marketing support costs to a minimum level so as to maximise cash flow for a short period before closing down;
   - *niche specialisation* by concentrating entirely on a very limited market segment which appears to show the most promise.

4. You may find yourself in charge of a *Wild Cat* in a market which has a high rate of growth but in which you have only a small market share. The experience curve theory implies poor profit margins but the market growth rate demands more and more cash. Strategy options are:
   - either invest heavily to attract an increased share of new users, and move into the 'Star' box; or
   - if there is not enough cash, get out of the race; or
   - look for a profitable niche.

Dangers in strategy decisions

Nevertheless, as many commentators have pointed out since this analytical tool was invented, there are a few major dangers of which to beware:

1. An over-concentration on cash flow considerations which may be simply short-term problems.
2. Problems of measurement of both share and growth and specific identification of the market:
   - should the definition of the product market be broad (cigarettes) or narrow (medium-priced filters)?
   - how much market segmentation, ie how detailed should the segments be – relative to market share?
   - should the concentration be on the total market or on the market served (are opportunities being overlooked)?
   - what geographical boundaries should be used – local, national, regional, international?
3. There may be limitations on the key assumptions involved in both the experience curve phenomenon (where the curve flattens out cost differences are small) and the market growth rate (entry barriers may be high enough to enhance margins or price competition may depress margins).

Even so the analysis has been used in forecasting future cash flow generation (see Figure 4.3) and also in international markets where the same product may encounter different market share/market growth situations both current and expected.

Future investment decisions

If the product portfolio analysis has to do with cash flow (generation and use) then the other major matrix (known variously as the General Electric or McKinsey matrix) has to do with investment decisions. [By investment the product manager is concerned with the amount of money and support which should or should not be given to her product line.]

By simplifying the process (which can become very complicated) down to two sets of factors, the following forms the basic design of the analysis:

Basic matrix   –   two-dimensional
Vertical axis   –   market attractiveness
Horizontal axis   –   business position.

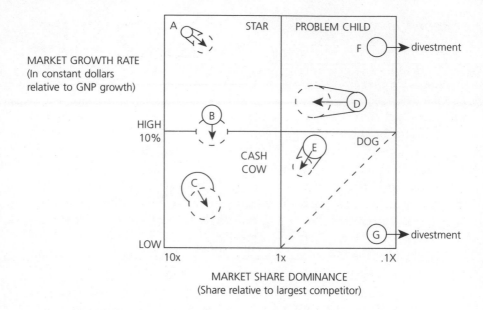

Figure 4.3 *Portfolio development over five years*

The chart is divided into nine boxes showing that, where market attractiveness and business position are high, investment, new or continued, is desirable and that where they are both low, disinvestment should take place. In the middle there should be a 'rethink'.

The process is as follows:

1. Identify the factors making for an attractive market (see Table 4.3).
2. Establish your business position factors – those which your manager colleagues think are essential aspects of your investment (see Table 4.3).
3. Get agreement among managers as to factors.
4. Make a priority list and give each a weighting (as a percentage is the easiest starting-point).
5. Measure each factor – by market research, internal discussion or external information.
6. Apply the weighting to the measurement and arrive at a total.
7. Apply totals (see Table 4.3) to the matrix (Figure 4.4).
8. Start a discussion on what the figures show.

Table 4.3 *Market attractiveness and business position measurement model*

	Weight (%x)	Measurement	Value
Market attractiveness			
Overall size	0.20	4.00	0.80
Annual growth	0.20	5.00	1.00
Historical margins	0.15	4.00	0.60
Competitive intensity	0.15	2.00	0.30
Technological requirements	0.15	3.00	0.45
Inflationary vulnerability	0.05	3.00	0.15
Energy requirements	0.05	2.00	0.10
Environmental Impact	0.05	1.00	0.05
Social/political/legal	Must be acceptable		–
	1.00		3.45
Business strength			
Market share	0.10	2.00	0.20
Share growth	0.15	4.00	0.60
Product quality	0.10	4.00	0.40
Brand reputation	0.10	5.00	0.50
Distribution network	0.05	3.00	0.15
Promotional effectiveness	0.05	2.00	0.10
Productive capacity	0.05	3.00	0.15
Productive efficiency	0.05	2.00	0.10
Unit costs	0.15	3.00	0.45
Material supplies	0.05	5.00	0.25
R&D performance	0.10	4.00	0.80
Managerial personnel	0.05	4.00	0.20
	1.00		3.50

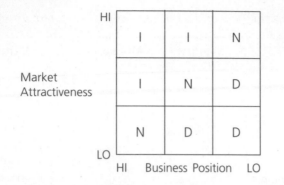

Figure 4.4 *Investment matrix*

CASE HISTORY

Product Background music
Market Recommended for investment – Belgium (and more specifically Brussels)

Attractiveness factors	Information available?	Scale of importance
Market size	Yes	1
Current coverage	No	2
Competition	Yes	3
Current systems	Yes	4
Social aspects	No	5
Legal aspects	Yes	6

Business strength factors	Five-point measurement		Weighting	Value
Market share	2	X	5	10
Product quality	4	X	15	60
Brand reputation	5	X	10	50
Distribution network (cable radio)	5	X	15	75
Promotional effectiveness	2	X	10	20
Costs	3	X	5	15
Personnel	2	X	10	20
			70	250

Possible total 350

= 71%

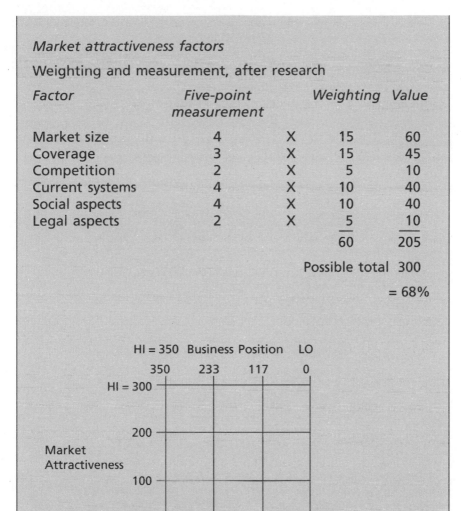

Market attractiveness factors

Weighting and measurement, after research

Factor	Five-point measurement		Weighting	Value
Market size	4	X	15	60
Coverage	3	X	15	45
Competition	2	X	5	10
Current systems	4	X	10	40
Social aspects	4	X	10	40
Legal aspects	2	X	5	10
			60	205

Possible total 300

= 68%

HI = 350 Business Position LO

350   233   117   0

HI = 300

200

Market Attractiveness

100

0

LO

Figure 4.5 *Investment matrix scales*

The next stage was to use the matrix to compare present markets with Belgium as a potential investment, by using the same basis. It was agreed to invest in Belgium, after discussion which emphasised the influence of the company's existing strengths.

CHECKLIST

The careful look at the product

- ■ Has the product range been examined?
- ■ Have you a specific checklist for this examination?
- ■ Are changes planned? By whom? When?
- ■ How does your product compare with that of competitors?
- ■ How do you know? Who has been questioned?
- ■ Do you know what your potential customers expect?
- ■ How do they buy? How do they see the product?
- ■ How is your 'differential advantage' created and maintained?
- ■ What sort of strategy are you following with your product?
- ■ Is the strategy directed by cash generation or the need for investment?
- ■ Are you in charge of a 'Dog' or a 'Star'?
- ■ Do your strategies take this into account?
- ■ Does your product deserve investment?
- ■ If so, how do you know?

5

Developing the Product Plan: Strengths and Weaknesses

SWOT ANALYSIS

'No rest for the wicked' – not even for the most virtuous product manager. Although this book tries to avoid describing theory, this chapter has to step back and look at a couple of 'views' of marketing which may help product managers to examine strengths and weaknesses in the whole marketing area.

Indeed the newly-appointed product manager – or the product manager who has been in the job for a few years and wants to refresh his ideas – may need to examine the basic business definition because it will certainly apply to his product. It will also be the basis of any examination of strengths and weaknesses (a SWOT analysis – which often overlooks the 'opportunities and threats' half of the process). Just as the definition of the company or organisation's business needs to be detailed and precise, so too does the definition of the product manager's product or service.

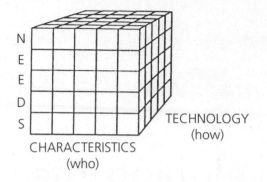

Figure 5.1 *Product definition axes*

PRODUCT DEFINITION

The definition of the product can be seen as a cube (see Figure 5.1) plus what might be called 'the product's operational axis'. The cube has three important dimensions in the process of definition:

1. Dimension 1 is the *needs and preferences of customers*. The product manager may well describe these in terms of the benefits provided, even the next stage of the customers' needs (a second television set, a third car, more television stations to watch, more holiday destinations, more cash point machines, etc).
2. Dimension 2 would be *customer characteristics*. In Chapter 3 characteristics were shown as one of the axes in a segmentation matrix. The characteristics in this dimension need to be defined equally carefully.
3. Dimension 3 identifies the *technology used*. In manufactured goods it might cover the raw materials used or manufacturing methods or technologies (such as electronics). In services such as training, it might cover distance training, programmed learning, interactive video or personal tutoring.

The aim of this analysis (perhaps 'deconstruction' is a better word) is to clarify the directions in which the product might go in the future.

For example, the product manager might suggest searching for more customers with the same needs (agricultural machinery to Eastern European countries, training services to different industries) – an expansion policy which would involve looking for customers with similar needs (including price levels) wherever they could be found.

Alternatively, he might decide that the most positive aspect of his product/market is the quality of the relationship with certain types of customer (a very evident example of this has been the rise of the garage forecourt shop, where petrol companies and garage owners provide their customers (characteristics = motorists) with an opportunity to purchase all kinds of emergency supplies, items to keep children quiet, flowers and chocolates as gifts or to assuage guilt, 'macho' encouragers like 'go-faster strips' and rear window messages – all of which are clearly aimed at the particular characteristics of those purchasing their major service: that of being a petrol filling station).

The technology dimension needs an accurate answer to the question 'How do we solve the customer's problem!' (with electronics companies it could be by means of a black box, or the installation of a total system, an advisory service or a 'menu' from which the client can choose). Careful identification is required so as to enable the product manager to identify precisely what the product or service's strengths are. Thus one area of development has been the franchising of operations. (It is expected that by the year 2000 franchising will account for 30 per cent of retail sales volume. Franchise Development Services publish a directory of over 1000 companies who operate franchises.) More simply, if your product is an infra-red control mechanism, future development might well be to seek out other controls that might be operated by infra-red beams.

PRODUCT'S OPERATIONAL AXIS

This is sometimes called the value-added system and describes the process from raw material via finished product to eventual customer. The product manager needs to identify two considerations:

1. where does his product fit along the axis;
2. how should he try to control the other stages: should be 'make or buy'.

[*Examples:* Suppose your product is a humble capacitor which is used in quantity in television sets and other electronically operated products. You manufacture them from raw materials which are bought in. You sell them to television set assemblers. The television set makers sell their television sets to the public via their chain of wholesalers and retailers. Is there a way in which you can ensure that *your* capacitors will reach the public? You can manufacture television sets, you can operate as a wholesaler, you can open retail shops or you can contract out all these things. This is an extreme case. Marks & Spencer contract out the manufacture of their products with very tight specification and carry out all the other operations themselves. Burtons manufacture, own shops and sell. A local water company buys its water but carries out all the remaining operations itself, down to replacing tap washers.]

Decisions are about value added and making a profit therefrom and control of specification, quality and end-user satisfaction. This is the product manager's task.

ANALYSIS OF STRENGTHS AND WEAKNESSES

Three important warnings:

1. ask why you are doing it;
2. sort out key areas as a starting-point;
3. follow through the analysis to action.

The purpose of the SWOT analysis is to ensure that soundly based objectives are set. Objectives need to reinforce success, not prop up failure. They should build on strengths and eliminate weaknesses.

What are the key areas which the product manager must consider? Tick the ones which apply to your product responsibilities.

Tick		Strength	Weakness
☐	Product design		
☐	Product quality		
☐	Product features		
☐	Market size		
☐	Market information		
☐	Market coverage		
☐	Distribution coverage		
☐	Distribution quality		
☐	Product packaging		
☐	Communication strategy		
☐	Sales promotion operations		
☐	Advertising operations		
☐	Selling		

☐ Product costs
☐ Product profitability
☐ Product life cycle
☐ New product development

Strengths and weaknesses are internal and new and therefore the list above applies to current activity – where I have provided a key area. In order to derive objectives from this analysis the description of strengths and weaknesses must be exhaustive. It is no use just writing (as one product manager I knew did) 'OK' against market coverage or drawing (as another used to do) crescendo and diminuendo signs (< and >). Often the SWOT analysis will require a project group which may also prepare a report outlining the situation, proposing objectives and recommending action to remedy faults or to build on strengths.

Opportunities and threats, which are external and in the future, also require careful analysis. Just as in the SW part of the 'SWOT' great care is needed in the selection of key areas. Of course, they may be the same as the strength and weakness list but there may well be no opportunities or threats in some areas.

Try this list for a service:

Tick	Opportunity	Threat
☐ Service function		
☐ Alternatives/competition		
☐ Competitors		
☐ Market growth		
☐ Marketing information		
☐ Costs of operation		
☐ Quality of operators		
☐ Productivity development		
☐ Communication systems		
☐ Promotional media		

Two further aspects need to be taken into account by the product manager:

1. SWOT analysis must fit with the rest of the organisation's analytical activities (preparation for the annual business plan, perhaps).
2. An assessment of the external environment should precede any attempt to list opportunities and threats, which would include:

– social changes (more senior citizens, shorter skirts);
– economic changes (Pacific Rim growth);
– political changes (materialism versus democracy);
– technological changes (intelligent computers);
– industry and organisational changes (quality circles);

which might have an impact on the future of the product or service.

EXAMPLE OF PRODUCT DEVELOPMENT

Some years ago the ABC Company entered the transport of cash and bullion business, with armoured vans and security guards. The company decided that its strength lay in the security aspect of its business. It became a well-known brand in the provision of this service. It provided a service which fulfilled the need for security, for the safe handling and protection of property.

As a result of its brand name, it developed in two directions: physical protection of goods and property and secure transport of important packages.

The company concluded that its security brand was a handicap in its courier business so its product manager decided to change its name and brand image.

The success of the security brand led the company to make a SWOT analysis based on the possible expansion into:

■ guarding military installations;
■ managing pop concerts;
■ transporting criminals;
■ managing remand centres or prisons;
■ emptying and filling cash machines;
■ breeding and training guard dogs.

As an *exercise*, set out the key questions for a SWOT analysis for the ABC Company:

■ What strengths and weaknesses might be crucial?
■ What opportunities and threats need investigating?

Finally, SWOT analysis figures feature in much writing and discussion of marketing and product planning. Here is a checklist for three different types of product manager:

1. an industrial product manager;
2. a consumer good brand product manager;
3. a service product manager.

CHECKLIST

Industrial

▪ Has the product line's purpose been defined according to Figure 5.1?
▪ Where does it stand on the operational axis?
▪ Have make or buy decisions been considered recently?
▪ What are the key areas of your strengths and weaknesses?
▪ Have you made an assessment of the external environment as a basis for the analysis of opportunities and threats?
▪ Does your SWOT process contain objectives and action plans?

Consumer

▪ Has your brand been defined in terms of the needs it fulfils and its customers' characteristics?
▪ Does your information about the brand's market performance include not only volume and value per outlet but also user attitude and communication effectiveness?
▪ What key areas are established as bases for objectives and results?
▪ Who will be involved in analysing strengths and weaknesses?
▪ Do you regularly get up-to-date reviews of the external environment?
▪ Are your SWOT action plans realistic?

Service

▪ Do you provide your service to a carefully delimited market segment?
▪ Is your information system and database good enough to provide a view of customers' requirements – now and in the future?
▪ Have you listed the marketing factors which you control?
▪ Can you judge whether they are weak or strong?
▪ What competitors do you have – now and in the future?

6

Developing the Product Plan: The Marketing Mix

CHANNELS OF DISTRIBUTION

Product managers usually consider channels of distribution to be an extremely boring subject. For most businesses they are traditional, they change very slowly, they are very difficult to control and changing from one sort of channel to another is fraught with problems. Thus the subject is not only boring but dangerous!

THE MARKETING MIX

To put distribution channels into context for the product manager, it is best to relate them to the total marketing mix. The marketing mix is described usually as the four factors which affect the consumer and which are controllable by the business, namely:

1. *Product* – fitness, quality, natural market.
2. *Price* – cost, credit terms, discounts, etc.
3. *Promotion* – selling, advertising, branding, etc.
4. *Place* – availability, channels of distribution, delivery.

(A number of authorities nowadays want to add a fifth 'P' for People and an 'S' for Service. My own view is that people are involved in every aspect of the mix and that service must be the normal way of approaching clients, customers, users, etc.)

The *product* has been discussed in Chapter 4; the *promotion* is part of Chapter 7 and *price* is discussed in this chapter.

Distribution channels are the main ingredient in the *place* section of the marketing mix. Once again, the product manager should review the distribution arrangements regularly – whether she has just been appointed or has been producing a product for some time.

Any examination, however cursory, will reveal the fact that distribution channels in most trades are undergoing changes – in many cases whole stages of distribution are being eliminated. Figure 6.1 demonstrates some of the patterns of distribution that exist with

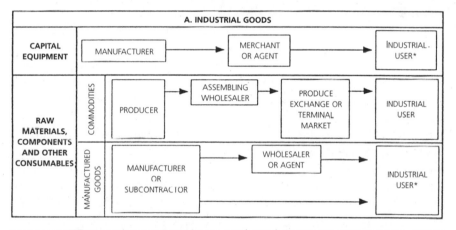

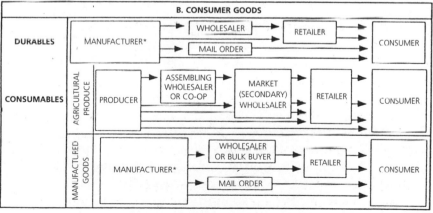

*These may be the same manufacturer.

Figure 6.1 *Distribution channels*

industrial goods and raw materials, with consumer goods both durables and consumables. It is noticeable that direct relationships between producer and consumer are shown in every case. The very existence of a pattern of distribution depends on the needs of the market and the willingness of businesses to understand it.

Channels of distribution for services are equally varied. Airlines, for example, use travel agents, tour operators and their own reservation systems to distribute their product. Banks use their own branches; insurance companies use agents or contact customers directly; fast-food outlets use franchise holders.

EXAMINATION OF YOUR CURRENT SYSTEM

Prior to an examination of the current system it is worthwhile to distinguish between channels of distribution and channels of selling. Confusion often arises because the manufacturer thinks that a distributor will also sell his or her product (eg most supermarkets will provide shelf space for a national brand – but it has to sell itself). Many airlines spend much time and money trying to persuade agents to sell their product. Distributors of electronic components provide their clients with the availability of a wide range of components produced by many manufacturers. A number of questions need to be asked.

1. What is the purpose of each link in the chain between the manufactured product or available service and the potential customer/user?
2. Do we have objectives for our channels? If so, what are they? (Costs, through put, sales, customer satisfaction?)
3. What are the costs, gross and net margins at each stage of the distribution process?
4. Have our distributors the advantage of a monopoly or semi-monopoly position – standard prices, dominant geographical position (eg the former Milk Marketing Board)?
5. Can we use other (unorthodox) distribution systems?
6. What are the costs (to you) of the current system of distribution:
   - working capital required to finance stocks;
   - cost of technical and training support to distributors;
   - cost of direct customer service?
7. Can we get nearer to the client/customer/consumer?
   - Is there a concentration of users and retail outlets – if so, should we sell direct?

- Does the distributor need to provide service or can it be done better by us directly?
- Can the distributor handle the need for credit?

[For example, the motor car trade is a franchise operation, in which the manufacturer controls the distribution, sales, credit and service operations closely, using its franchise to sell both its own and other acceptable accessories. The principal usually establishes targets for sales and provides training, national advertising and support for local promotions.]

8. What about physical distribution of goods?
   - Dependent on the life of the product and methods of change?
   - What about damage and waste in transit?
   - Compare cost of direct distribution (overnight packages, air freight, etc) with the establishing of local warehouses.
   - Cost, speed, reliability, liability to pilferage, etc of various alternatives?

STOCK LEVELS AND 'JUST-IN-TIME'

Control over distribution systems has been affected much in recent years by the pressure to reduce stock levels and to substitute a just-in-time (JIT) method of delivery. The advantages of the JIT approach depend on where you are on the product's operational axis. The nearer your business is to the end user the greater the advantage; further back along the manufacturing/production chain more effort is required. (In process industries, such as chemicals and oil or food, there seems to be great difficulty in making the system work at all.)

'JIT is a series of manufacturing and supply chain techniques that aim to slash inventory levels and improve customer service by manufacturing not only at the exact time the customer requires, but also in the exact quantity he actually needs,' writes Wheatley. On the plus side it is an approach to manufacturing management that demonstrates not only that manufacturing companies can be run without buffer stocks ('just-in-case') but that they can be run more effectively. On the minus side it can mean that the stockholding function is pushed back in the chain and fewer suppliers are prepared to stand the costs of stockholding.

The action that needs to be taken results from the answers to the question 'Why are stocks held?' Answers such as:

■ length of set-up time;
■ suppliers' suspect quality;
■ suppliers' uncertain deliveries;

need to be looked at carefully to see whether the cost of the problem is greater or less than the cost of the solution (namely, costs of service, costs of scrapping and costs of warehouse space).

The product manager's input into this problem must start from the customer's requirement and from the solving of the customer's problem. If the customer demands a JIT delivery system, then the product manager has to set in motion the changes in factory lay-out, quality control and supply sources which can enable the production operation to satisfy the customer. [*Note:* Assumptions about customer requirements can cause unnecessary expense, for example assuming that *every* customer needs next-day delivery. They can also cause lost orders, for example assuming that *all* customers carry sufficient stocks to keep their own production line going. Customer requirements must be researched and checked carefully.]

CHANNELS OF SELLING

The channels of selling, for very many businesses and for almost all services, remain an integral part of the business itself (exceptions might be insurance companies working through building societies, BT's phone cards sold by stationery shops). Thus the product manager needs to look carefully at her selling channels – particularly where she finds a lethargic and uninterested channel (an accusation often levelled at the wholesaler/distributor, who may often carry too many lines to be able to give sufficient attention to each). Two courses of action may be followed:

1. Go direct – which may involve developing new brand loyalties, training of a salesforce, establishing guarantees of quality and entering the dangerous world of retail pricing.
2. Undertake 'back selling' – establishing a sales activity which promotes the product or service to the end user/client/customer but which directs the order to the distributor or wholesaler who undertakes the delivery of the goods. (This method of reinforcing the local distributor was used frequently by USA companies starting up in Europe.) This can work in many fields where

selling the product can be controlled separately and the delivery of the product is a distinct activity with its own specialisms.

So first check:

■ agents – how long appointed, level of turnover;
■ distributors – type of agreement, volume sold;
■ wholesalers – quality, turnover, margin, effort;
■ competitors – methods of distribution, sales channels;
■ changes in channels and trends.

EXAMPLE

The Institute of Grocery Distribution published the following information in 1991:

	1981 (£m)	1989 (£m)	1990 (£m)
Wholesale sales at current prices			
Cash and carry	3,168	7,454	7,855
Delivered trade	1,823	3,496	2,527

showing that cash and carry depots' sales increased from 63.5 per cent of the total in 1981 to 75.7 per cent in 1990.

Nielsen reported that in the grocery trade the number of shops in 1971 was 105,283 but by 1991 it had reduced to 48,207; and that the number of independents had shrunk from 42.5 per cent in 1971 to 13.9 per cent in 1991.

Unfortunately changes in industrial patterns of distribution and the rise and fall of service businesses are not researched in such detail – though information about consumers' behaviour patterns is often detailed in the General Household Survey and, for example, the Society of Motor Manufacturers and Traders note that in 1970 the percentage of imported cars in new registrations was 14.3 per cent – by 1991 it had risen to a staggering 55.7 per cent. (Could affect a garage owner's choice of franchise!)

■ Create criteria for judging distribution systems.
■ Regularly check the success or failure of the distributor.
■ Agree objective, targets and help required all down the line.

PRICING AND DISCOUNT STRUCTURES

Since the end of resale price maintenance which enabled manufacturers to dictate the pricing of their products right through to the consumer, the channel of distribution has also become a channel of pricing policy.

The importance of pricing as an element in the marketing mix varies from one company to another. In this not only do the industry structure and the size of the firm play a role but also the importance of price, in buying decision of the customer.

By structure I mean the spectrum from perfect competition (if such a state can ever be said to exist) where supply and demand only influence the price, to monopoly where the price is set by the sole supplier. [Industry structure arguments have been modified by the establishing of privatised monopolies whose pricing is subject only to the view (whim, interference?) of a regulator.]

So, first the product manager must position her product. Is it a leader? Can she initiate price changes and expect other smaller firms to follow suit? (Has she a 'Cash Cow' product, therefore?) Or is the product an also-ran? Has the price got to be fixed in relation to the leader's decision?

Second, she must establish, as I have indicated, the importance of price as a reason to buy or a reason not to buy in relation to the other factors in the marketing mix (see Chapter 7). For example, if the price level is crucial to the buyer's decision, then this increases the pressure to set a price level which will move the required volume of product or which will provide the targeted profit. The pressures on the price level setting are very strong and the product manager may need help in trying to do the right thing (see Table 6.1).

Table 6.1 *Price level setting pressures*

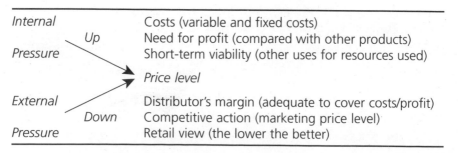

Generally, external pressure is towards lowering the price and internal pressure is towards raising it.

As we shall see in Chapter 8, pricing also varies according to the stage in the life cycle that the product has reached; and is influenced by the way in which the marketing budget is set up. For example, if the price is the major influencing factor then resources should be pumped in so as to keep the price down.

Additionally – although the product manager rarely has any say in these areas – the price will be influenced by all kinds of sales and payment motivators and credit agreements.

Purchasing managers will negotiate for better credit terms (payment within 60 days rather than 30 days) discounts for quantity, discounts for prompt payment (2.5 per cent for payment within 30 days) and retrospective rebates for quantity (rebates on the total bill which occur when the client has purchased more than a specified amount within, say, a year). All these act as distortions on the price. The month-end figures will reflect the real price rather than the price-list price!

CHECKLIST

■ How important are distribution decisions – for you, for the customer?
■ Can you influence distributors' activities?
■ Have you looked at the cost of distribution – within the end price to the consumer? Can it be reduced?
■ To what extent are your distributors also channels of selling?
■ Can you influence their sales activity? Do you?
■ Have you forecast changes in distribution patterns?
■ Will you need to change in the next five years?

7

Developing the Product Plan: Communicating with Customers

MODELS OF CONSUMER BEHAVIOUR

Models of industrial activity, enterprise and innovation usually take what might be called the 'eureka' form. They assume that the inventor, innovator or entrepreneur has an idea or creates a product as a result of insight into customers' requirements or perhaps research into customers' needs. The remainder of the model follows from this – via manufacture, customer persuasion to delivery and follow-up service. I believe that more meaningful models should be created of consumer/customer behaviour which can give insight into what action industrialists and marketers ought to take. In this chapter I consider the need for models and types of models; I then outline a general model of consumer behaviour and the lessons to be drawn from it, in particular for the product manager.

NEED FOR MODELS

The need for models arises in three directions:

1. In thinking about consumers everyone makes a large number of assumptions which need to be examined and put in order if they are to be a guide to planned action.
2. If a model is created there then exists something concrete which describes consumer behaviour. It can be discussed, modified where necessary, or it may be used as a basis for action.
3. A theoretical model is generally sufficiently flexible to cover different situations and allow those situations to be studied within a stable framework.
4. In addition, since it is not possible to examine real situations scientifically and subject them to tests, we need to examine representations of real situations to look at the influence of internal and external events on them.

TYPES OF MODEL

There are three main types of model which can be used to make marketing discussions more valuable. Each of the three types can have further ramifications, of course, depending on whether the situation being modelled is capable of further development.

Simple assumptions

This type of model is used all the time and is based on folk history, accepted beliefs and what Galbraith calls 'conventional wisdom'. A typical example of such a model is the assumption that reducing the price of a product automatically increases its sales. Another well-known example is Emerson's model that 'if a man . . . makes a better mouse-trap, the world will make a beaten path to his door'. This takes no account of other methods of eliminating mice, whether the mice think it is a better mousetrap or how the world gets to know about the improvement in the product. Such models are only too prevalent and are used to support decisions in all parts of a business. The main criticism to be offered is that, for the most part, they are not subject to critical review because they are unspoken.

Step models (or stage by stage models)

These models are used for teaching and illustration purposes, being capable of clear visualisation. For this type of model a process of action is split up into its component parts and external or internal influences are introduced so that a stylised picture is drawn. This copies the patterns drawn by method study engineers, system analysts or network planners but is applied to assumed activities or states of mind of consumers. They can be seen as 'process diagrams' applied to consumer behaviour.

Mathematical/calculus models

Having created a process diagram or a step model, research can turn much of what is shown into mathematical equations. Particularly when optimum solutions are needed to linear programming or other operations research problems, calculus or other mathematical techniques can be applied. Theories of probability and multiple regression analysis are favourite instruments for producing solutions in difficult or uncertain models of behaviour. A major criticism is that they produce an apparent certainty (a finite number) where no real certainty exists. As a result they can be misleading.

GENERAL MODELS OF CONSUMER BEHAVIOUR

I have developed a general model of consumer behaviour under three headings – mass consumers of merchandise, industrial consumers and consumers of services. Such models are likely to generalise but (1) they will indicate ways in which they can be further refined; and (2) they can indicate appropriate action on the part of those who wish to intervene; for example, if you wish to inform your potential market of your product's existence, its price or its availability, you would wish to use different channels or media at different stages of the model, to affect different aspects of consumer's behaviour.

General consumer (mass market)

By necessity most models show a chronological sequence – though naturally the process can be a circular one, that is, the consumer can be at any stage in the model and also can start again at the beginning in relation to an existing 'satisfaction' (see Table 7.1).

Table 7.1 *Mass market model*

Stage	Instrument
1. Happy existence/ignorance ▽	–
2. Dissatisfaction due to external influences ▽	Education Newspapers and magazines Friends with money
3. Seeks information ▽	The Internet Shops Advertisement, competition
4. Stimulated to action ▽	Salespeople, advertisements
5. Sampling of article ▽	Product quality Type of outlet
6. Experience ▽	Removing cognitive dissonance through advertisements
7. Satisfaction ▽	Happy reminders
8. Repeat purchase	Distribution levels (Competition)

Table 7.1 shows the process through which a typical consumer passes and the instruments of intervention in the process.

1. The initial state of happy existence or ignorance is likely to be changed into dissatisfaction through some kind of external influence. I suggest that this might come, in the short term, from friends, newspapers or perhaps from the availability of wealth.
2. Intervention by the manufacturer needs to be in the form of arousing dissatisfaction by suggesting life can be different – more comfortable, easier, more exciting, more interesting, more glamorous; executed through the media that reaches the potential customers – newspapers, magazines, television.
3. 'Seeking information' is covered by the information available in shops or advertisements and on the Internet. It is at this point that the product manager needs to take account of the competition; and to note that competition is only important in so far as the customer is aware of it. (For example: somewhere there may be a product which is twice as good and half the price of the

ones demonstrated. If the customer does not know of its existence then in effect it does not exist as a competitor.)

4. 'Stimulated to action' is the stage where intervention by advertising and salespeople is at its strongest. The product manager needs strongly to influence both advertising and selling activity at this point, which is very difficult in a self-service situation, such as a supermarket. (Hence the need for good packaging, merchandising and sales promotion.)

Stages 5, 6, 7 and 8 are very often underestimated. Their importance lies in the reinforcement of customer satisfaction with the product.

Industrial consumer

Similar stages and instruments can be identified for industrial customers – they can be more or less sophisticated. For example, the whole new area of vendor evaluation can be separated from the decision-making process as can be seen from Table 7.2.

'Environmental stimulus' can be assisted by good public relations (PR) in the form of articles, seminars, exhibition invitations, etc. 'Internal stimulus' to change can be triggered by advertising, eg in magazines read by top management. 'Decision to change product or system' will be signalled by salespeople and stimulated by sales promotion.

The product manager must be aware of and try to manage the different instruments – even if they are not directly under his control. As can be seen from Table 7.2, the product manager is one of the instruments directly involved.

Services

As an example of a consumer model for the use of services I have taken the holiday product, which shows a similar pattern of stages and instruments of intervention. It must be remembered that if you as producer wish to influence the potential consumer then you must apply the appropriate instrument at the right place and time. In this model it is to be noted that competition varies depending on the stage (Table 7.3).

One can note that at the first stage competition involves doing nothing, staying at home, buying a video recorder or saving money. At the second stage, competition involves country A, country B, country C, package holiday, own car, coach, etc. At the experience

Table 7.2 *Industrial market model*

Stage	Instrument
1. Existing production ▽	Sales visits
2. Environmental stimulus ▽	PR – seminars
3. Internal stimulus	Product manager Advertising, competition
4. Decision to change system or product ▽	Salespeople Sales promotion
5. Vendor evaluation ▽	Product manager Product quality
6. Purchase decision ▽	'Image' – negotiator
7. Testing, prototype, manufacture ▽	Applications engineer
8. Satisfaction ▽	Service, follow-up
9. Follow-on orders	Salespeople

Table 7.3 *Service market model*

Stage	Instrument
1. External pressure to take a holiday ▽	PR in magazines
2. Seeking information ▽	Advertisement in newspapers Information in travel agencies Brochures
3. Decision making Choice and selection ▽	Advertisement on television Holiday programmes on television Brochure, free telephone lines
4. Holiday booking ▽	Agency/administration staff Forms, telephone handling
5. Experience ▽	Couriers at resort
6. Word-of-mouth	Follow-up by agents

stage, competition is other hotels at the resort. At each stage it must be measured and confronted.

LESSONS FOR PRODUCT MANAGERS

There are four major lessons which follow from the reasoning above. These apply to both strategy and action on the part of companies which wish to profit by providing customer satisfaction.

Assessing customer behaviour

Since the desired outcome is that the customer gains satisfaction by using our product the models show, by their crudity, the need for research by individual companies into how their customers actually behave. A general model can be used as a framework but the product manager needs quantitative details, for example as to how many customers can take a particular sort of action at any time, or how long the process of decision making takes. [The personal computer market shows the need for firm information as to quantities and timing. It is also incidentally a good example of everybody watching his or her competitor!]

Selection of appropriate strategy

Models are about both strategy and action. The accurate assessment of the behaviour of customers provides the possibility of selecting a strategy which is both appropriate to the current situation and profitable. Such strategies can be either reactive or proactive. For example, a large company can either follow in the wake of customer behaviour, noting the well-known breakdown of behavioural types into: 2.5 per cent innovators, 16 per cent early adopters, 34 per cent early majority, etc and arrange to meet the requirements of the early majority; or it can try to influence the innovators (eg e-mail, Internet, compact disc) and thus pre-empt action by others.

Getting the right organisation

Intervening, as suggested earlier, in models of consumer behaviour also demands the organisation which will enable a company to do this. This will necessarily vary to fit with how the company's consumers behave both in terms of command and control. In certain circumstances the variation between one market and another is so great (in terms of timing, quantities, expectations) that it would not be possible to manage them all under one grouping. In other cases it may be wisest to manage the product as a total division even though it covers a wide variety of market behaviour patterns.

Lessons for product managers

The major lessons which become evident from the above discussion are the need for product managers to make colleagues aware of the subtleties of using models to plan behaviour. Current strategic thinking (marketing as warfare, market share and market growth, etc) tends to look at the behaviour of other companies in the market. Consumer models turn the view *outwards*; this should be the emphasis in the exercise of product management, ie the interpretation of the market to the company!

FACTORS INVOLVED, WEIGHTING AND APPLYING

Not only do customers/consumers/clients/buyers proceed via a series of steps towards their purchasing decision but they are also influenced to different degrees by the different factors of the marketing mix. Each market segment reacts in its own way. Product managers need to analyse this before planning their communication strategy:

1. Establish the profile of each market segment (see Chapter 3).
2. List the factors which are under your control (or at least the ones you can influence) such as:
   - the product design and technology;
   - the price level, payment reductions, etc;
   - the promotion – advertising, PR selling, brand;
   - the place – channels, availability;
   - the service – speed, cost.
3. Create a matrix with segments on the horizontal axis and the factors on the vertical axis (as in Figure 7.1).
4. Assess the impact of each factor (on a scale of one to five) on the separate market segments.

Market Segments

Factors	A 1	2	3	4	5	B 1	2	3	4	5	C 1	2	3	4	5	D 1	2	3	4	5
PRODUCT																				
Design																				
Technology																				
PRICE																				
Basic																				
Credit																				
PROMOTION																				
Advertising																				
PR																				
Selling																				
'Brand'																				
PLACE																				
Availability																				
Channels																				
SERVICE																				
Speed																				
Cost																				

Figure 7.1 *Marketing mix factors*

The result will provide:

■ a profile of the expected effectiveness of each factor on a given sector;
■ an indication of how resources (money, management time and effort) should be allocated;
■ a starting-point for the budget;
■ an area where market research can fill in the details or validate hypotheses.

THE ADVERTISING BRIEF

The product and the price have been discussed in earlier chapters. One of the major functions of the product manager addressed here is the choice of, and relationship with, his selected advertising agency. He may already have chosen an agency. There may be one which the company has employed for years. To get the best out of an agency it is worthwhile recognising what it can do, basic selection and working with an agency on the brief.

An agency can provide three things for a client – advice, creation and execution. On the advisory side it can help in drawing up the marketing plan by providing both new research and old knowledge, by finding out where the advertising opportunity exists and by bringing to bear the agency's own marketing experience with other clients and in other fields, in such areas as product and pack testing and programming of advertising releases.

As for creation, and this is the area in which an advertising agency usually excels, the list of items which an agency can write or design includes:

1. Advertising by:
   - posters;
   - television and press;
   - films and videos;
   - radio;
   - direct mail.
2. Premium offers:
   - gift schemes;
   - competitions.
3. Showcards:
   - merchandising aids;
   - stands, dispensers;
   - showroom displays;
     mobile exhibitions;
   - shops-within-shops.
4. Sales material such as:
   - leaflets;
   - booklets;
   - catalogues;
   - price lists;
   - sales kits for salespeople.
5. Packaging and 'image' material such as:
   - letter headings;
   - wrappers;
   - packs;
   - van designs;
   - house style generally.

The agency itself is responsible for issuing some of the material it creates but in addition it produces artwork, films, photographs and posters. It gets film made and sent to publishers. It oversees printing and direct mail arrangements and can organise competitions and gift schemes. It is also usually responsible for checking advertising by obtaining voucher copies of publications and monitoring television advertising.

The product manager has a very large responsibility in many businesses both in selecting the right agency for his product and briefing the agency staff adequately. In a recent discussion, a very wise advertising man gave this advice to those looking for an agency.

'First, the size of the agency should match, roughly, the size of the marketing operation. Large agencies are often organised on a cellular basis, rather like an agglomeration of small agencies and a small to medium-sized client may become either overwhelmed or overlooked by the large agency. A list should be made after advice has been sought and after picking out advertisements that particularly appeal to you in journals and finding out which agencies are responsible for them.

Secondly, from the list that has been drawn up, select the agencies that have some knowledge of the market in which your goods are sold. This is necessary in consumer goods – the furniture trade is quite different from the food trade, for example – but in industrial selling it is essential. Buying from the agency, after all, is employing someone with expertise in the market; you have the product expertise yourself.

Thirdly, try to get some evaluation of the shortlist from acquaintances and contacts in other trades and other companies before arranging to meet the agency personnel.

Fourthly, once you show interest in an agency you will be invited to a presentation. Remember that a presentation is a sales pitch – the agency is trying to sell you its services. Remember, too, that you are hoping to work closely with the people who are making the presentation. While you are looking at what they can do, it is important to try to assess what they *are*. The agency/client relationship will founder if it rests on the basis simply of the agency having successfully sold itself to the client.

Finally, it is wise to arrange for the first period to be a probationary one, for both parties. Clients change agencies quite often – generally for very good reasons – but occasionally because the selection was a mistake.'

Once an agency has been selected it should become part of the marketing team. As part of the team it should receive a good briefing. This is the most important contribution that can be made to the successful use of the agency. The briefing may result from a series of meetings with the agency, talking round the advertising and promotion problems. Eventually it should be committed to paper and should comprise:

1. Marketing objectives:
   - share of market, present and aimed for;
   - distribution policy;
   - pricing policy;
   - sales resources committed;
   - patterns of consumption, use, etc, where known;
   - advertising/promotion appropriation.
2. Product details:
   - history of product and stage of life;
   - methods of manufacture;
   - pack sizes, packaging, transport and distribution, shelf life;
   - after-sales service;
   - technical requirements.
3. Advertising and promotion policy:
   - 'straight' advertising;
   - 'gimmicks';
   - special promotional aids/merchandising;
   - press and public relations;
   - image building;
   - competitive position.
4. Image it is desired to present:
   - relating to the product itself;
   - relating to the company.
5. Programme of important dates:
   - exhibitions;
   - seasons;
   - new product launches, designs, patterns.

The agency should then be able to submit a plan showing proposals for the advertising campaign for the next period – a year or 18 months, perhaps two years – which should tie in with the marketing plan.

DATABASE MARKETING

The computer has entered the fray. It is said that if a customer requires a particular specification of the product then computer assisted manufacture (CAM) can produce it for him or her within 24 hours, provided that the information about his or her likely requests is already captured on the database. (I reckon this will occur with some regularity from 2025 onwards!)

However there is a serious point here for the product manager. He has to keep (and update regularly) the maximum amount of information about individual customers in an accessible database. It is no use simply having a computerised Christmas card list!

More and more emphasis is placed on needing to provide service to the customer and provide for him or her exactly what is required. Additionally if you have detailed information about a client you can approach him or her with precisely the right message at the right time about the right product. Direct marketing (direct mail) aimed at that segment of the market which the product manager has been able to pinpoint is becoming more and more dominant. The information needed in the database is:

■ Name, address and size of firm, company, organisation.
■ Name and function of individual.
■ Contacts with company – dates.
■ Contacts with individual – dates.
■ Reason for contacts.
■ Outcome of contacts:
   – results;
   – orders (volume/value);
   – views.
■ Profitability of organisation's relationship.
■ Other members of the decision-making unit:
   – user – name/function;
   – influencer – name/function;
   – decision maker – name/function;
   – gatekeeper – name/function;
   – contacts/referrals/relationships (with other possible customers/clients);
   – market segment – characteristics
                     – motivations;
   – direct mail contact – effectiveness;
   – competitors' relationship – volume/value
                     – second source, etc

SELLING AND SALESPEOPLE

The product manager has at least four contact points with selling and salespeople. (In some businesses he has to be a salesman as well; in which case he needs some comprehensive sales training!)

Collection of information

Since the salespeople are those closest to actual customers and clients, they are often the best (and sometimes the only) source of information about how customers behave and think. In collecting information from salespeople the product manager will naturally sell the idea to the sales manager first of all. He should have a clear idea of what information he wants to obtain (it is useful to create a questionnaire). He should also make clear that the information he is seeking is not designed to be part of the measurement of sales performance or an assessment of the respondent's ability. (I do not need to add necessity of 'please' and 'thank you' – even though these little courtesies are sometimes forgotten. The product manager needs to sell harder in a more difficult environment than that met by most salespeople.)

The sort of information which he can get only from the salesforce is as follows:

▓ Which factors among the marketing mix impresses the client most?
▓ How does the product, price, promotion, delivery and service compare with competition (on a scale of one to five)?
▓ Which factor needs most improvement?
▓ What are the trends in purchasing by the clients?
▓ How have recent changes (product design, advertising, sales promotion, price, etc) been received by the customer?

Outlining the sales story

As a result of successful information collection (and therefore knowledge of the market) the product manager often has the responsibility of developing the sales story of his product. Therefore he needs to understand how clients/customers think and the way in which sales are made. It is not enough merely to list what care and attention has gone into the manufacture of a product, nor what technological marvels are built into the way it operates; nor will it do to explain that the business has been established since 1890!

The sales story – and the same applies whether it is a tangible product or an intangible service – should have the following features:

1. Customer (user, client) problems which the product solves.
2. Technical description of the product or service.
3. Applications of the product or service.
4. Benefits, ie what the customer will get from the product or service.
5. Features which back up the promise inherent in the benefits.
6. Back-up, namely, price, promotion, branding, service, follow-up.
7. Launch date, samples, competition, etc (for a new product).

Presentations

One of the tasks which almost all product managers must perform, regularly, is to make a presentation to salespeople of his product line (new product, new range or revamped service). Often such a presentation is part of a series. The product manager is in competition not only with other product managers but also with the advertising manager, the service manager and the sales manager! Product managers may have to present their latest new and improved offering to groups of distributors. [This could be the occasion of a large and impressive meeting when the company transports all its distributors to the shores of Lake Geneva, with product presentation as the serious excuse for the meeting.]

Whether the presentation is one with 24 slide projectors, video films and rock music or whether it is a simple meeting with a few colleagues and a flipchart the principles are the same. The presenter needs to be concerned with three vital matters:

1. *Planning and preparation* which involves deciding what result the presenter expects from his or her talk; how to make the subject matter interesting; what visual reinforcement will be needed.
2. *The audience* which needs to be taken into account in the subject matter, the method and technique. (Usually the audience are doing you a favour by giving up some of their time to listen to you.) A good rule is 'Never underestimate their intelligence, but never overestimate their knowledge'.

3. *Rehearsal* which helps both the speaker and the audience. It gives the speaker confidence both personal and in his or her visuals; the audience deserves nothing better than a fully rehearsed and professional presentation, without panics, hiccups or disasters!

Here is a short checklist on giving a talk, which product managers will find useful.

EXAMPLE

Giving a talk

Preliminary:

1. Are you clear on the topic?
2. What results will you try for?
3. What will the audience be?
4. Do you have time to make your point?
5. What sort of visual aids will you need?
6. Do you have time to prepare them?
7. Who is your contact person?

Material collection and arrangement:

1. Do you know where your material will come from?
   - Own resources?
   - Libraries?
   - Other people?
2. Do you have a notebook or small cards to write down ideas as they arise?
3. What are the main points? What are the main headings?
4. Have you laid out your talk in the same form as an 'organi-gram'?
5. Have you reduced the number of points you propose to make to a minimum?
6. What are you going to start with?
7. What sort of audience reaction do you expect?
8. Are you going to read your speech?
   - Memorise it and recite it?
   - Speak from detailed notes?
   - Speak from headings using cards or A4 sheets?
9. What are the first sentences of your talk?
   - Have you written them down?
   - Are you using a joke?

- Have you tried it out on a friend?
- Are you summarising the talk?
- Will you mention the objective?
- Will you state the theme in terms of the audience's benefit?
10. What are the last sentences of your talk?
    - Have you written them down?
    - Are you ending with a joke?
    - Are you asking a question?
    - Are you closing with a summary of what you have said?

Final preparation:

1. Are your notes typed clearly, double spaced?
2. Are your cards numbered?
3. Are they tied together with a lace through the hole in the corner or Treasury tag?
4. Have you timed your talk and marked the times?
5. How many times have you rehearsed it?
6. How many times have you rehearsed it?
7. How many times have you rehearsed it?

Delivery:

1. Stand up straight.
2. Do not jingle coins in your pockets.
3. Speak slowly at first.
4. Speak clearly.
5. Look at everyone.
6. Do not speak with your back to the audience.
7. Gesture naturally – as your enthusiasm demands.
8. Smile!
9. Pause after making important points.
10. Get the punch-line quotations right.
11. Courage!

Get No. 11 typed in capitals and put it on the lectern in front of you. Finally, a motto for all presenters, from Cervantes:

Study to explain your thoughts and set them in the truest light, taking great trouble not to let them remain dark and complicated, but clear and understandable.

Visits to customers

As demonstrated in the models of consumer behaviour earlier in this chapter, product managers need to visit customers from time to time. These visits must always be in the company of the salesperson who is responsible for that customer. (In many companies there is an ongoing problem of the 'two-person visit'.)

A visit (with a salesperson) has the following advantages:

- it demonstrates to the customer the high level of the company's interest in his/her views;
- it provides the product manager with an insight into the customer's purchasing behaviour;
- it enables the product manager to gain from the customer information which, for the customer, has no sales overtones;
- it gives the salesperson a contact with the product manager and can lead to a useful exchange of views;
- it can help the product manager to identify the benefits which the customer is seeking.

It is evidently more important for the product manager to visit customers either at an early stage in the product's life or at a stage when a new product is in development.

General rules for the two-person visit are as follows:

- warn the customer in advance;
- get agreement between product manager and salesperson on the shape of the discussion (who should talk about what!);
- explain clearly to the customer the purpose of the visit;
- do not confuse the customer by trying to sell when you are trying to gain information;
- do not denigrate competitors;
- try to avoid arguments about delivery and prices;
- have a clear objective in terms of information sought;
- discuss result afterwards with the salesperson.

CHECKLIST

■ Have you created a model of *your* consumer's behaviour process?
■ Can you use it in discussions with the different factors and their managers?
■ Have you sufficient information to create a factor analysis matrix like Figure 7.1?
■ Is your advertising agency working well for you – is it part of your marketing team?
■ Do you produce a clear brief for the agency each year?
■ Are your relations with salespeople:
  – harmonious;
  – useful;
  – neutral;
  – non-existent?
■ Are your presentations planned and rehearsed?
■ Do they help the audience?
■ Do you report regularly both to your boss and to the sales manager on your visits to customers?

8

The Product Life Cycle

A STRATEGIC INDICATOR

One aspect of her product which seems regularly to be used as a strategic indicator is the so-called 'product life cycle'. The concept originated long before sales managers were superseded by marketing managers – and when product managers had hardly been thought of. The idea persists, however, that the product goes through a life cycle of introduction, growth, maturity and decline – and therefore that strategic decisions should take account of the position of the product on its life cycle curve (Figure 8.1).

The cynical will point out that it is very easy after the event to plot the history of a product (the product's obituary?) but very difficult if not impossible to establish either its current position or its future development.

Before either using the concept or writing it off it is worthwhile to look at the history of the product. This will enable the product manager to create a picture of the product which may help to indicate what sort of actions are desirable. The following steps should be taken:

1. Identify whether the product is a *class* of product (eg cars) or a *form* of product (eg hatch-backs) or a *brand* (eg Rover). This is important because of the danger of comparing the performance of your brand with either of the other two and vice versa. (*Note:* cars as a class have gained sales; hatch-backs have lost; Rovers have fluctuating fortunes.)

2. Take each measure in turn – volume, turnover (revenue) and profitability (calculated as contribution or return on investment)

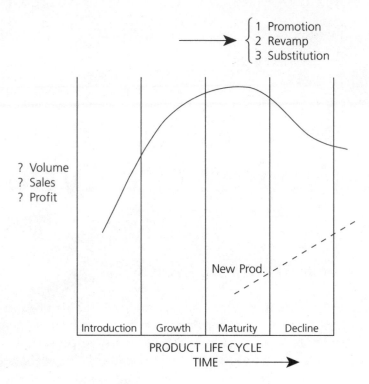

Figure 8.1 *Product life cycle*

– and check on the performance of each measure as far back as it
is useful to go (five years, ten years).
3. Plot the measures separately on a multiple chart and see what
has happened to the life cycle over those five years.
4. And what has happened to your major competitor's product.

If you are lucky the graphs you have sketched will demonstrate
where your product is in its life cycle. If it is clear then some of the
strategies shown in Table 8.1 may be appropriate.

The three strategies (promotion, revamp, substitution) suggested
when the product shows clear signs of decline need some
explanation. They are often sufficiently successful to enable the new
product (see Chapter 9) to get to the marketplace without an hiatus.
By *promotion* I include not only the obvious one of a new and more
powerful message to the chosen market segment but a simultaneous
reduction of the price level (or a 'get 20 per cent more for the same
price' action) and a special sales drive to give the customers a new
opportunity to buy. [One company puts together a special telesales
action directed towards current and past customers/clients.]

Table 8.1 Product cycle strategies

	Main strategy	Price	Advertising	Promotion
Introduction	Aim to get Innovators to try 'P'	Can it be high enough to cover launch costs?	Generate awareness of 'P'	Samples, test drives try out exercises
Growth	Aim at the wider market	Keep price up to take advantage of market growth	Benefit selling to the wider market. Reinforce success	Reduced promotion effort
Maturity	Fight off all the increasing competition Support your customers	Avoid price wars	Stress your differential advantages	Use promotions to attract users to try your brand
Decline	1. Promotion 2. Revamp	Reduce price Change price level drastically	Spend more Stress the change	Special offers Splash the changes
	3. Substitution	Price down to clear stocks	Advertise price	Do nothing

By *revamp* I mean more imaginative or creative packaging (in the case of services perhaps join the product with others in a new combined package – not only household insurance but a home emergency service to cover leaks and floods!) or redesign of a different feature, a switch or a handle.

By *substitution* I mean the development of a new product to take the place of the one in decline: it usually has to solve the same problem but in a slightly different way or even solve two or three problems at once. [A new service which is now offered was developed from simple lift maintenance to being a 'total management of the building' service because lifts became more and more reliable and required less maintenance.]

THE PRODUCT LIFE CYCLE AS A STRATEGIC PLANNING TOOL

To demonstrate the way in which the product life cycle can be made into a strategic planning tool I have outlined the case of the Italian crane, as handled by a colleague, Joe Cagnina.

EXAMPLE

The case of the Italian crane

Joe had lectured regularly at Management Centre Europe in Brussels on product management and, in particular, on the product life cycle. As a consultant he was asked to assist the Constructa SpA company in the development and marketing of their new crane.

He felt that the product life cycle might be used as a forecasting or strategy instrument provided:

1. activities before the launch were costed;
2. estimates covered not only sales, but also costs and profitability throughout the cycle.

After discussions with the different departments in the company he concluded that four stages could be identified (he called them 'action stages') including the launch, *before* the introduction stage in the product life cycle, and six stages of the product life cycle proper. These were:

1. *Search and screening of ideas*. A vitally important part of the process, which needed a great deal of organising, time and attention (which pointed to the need to establish the time required for each stage).
2. *Technical and marketing development*. This signalled the need for both developments to take place within the same time period.
3. *Testing of performance and of marketing*. Following naturally from development effort.
4. *Market launch*. At this point – if properly controlled – the whole activity can be brought to a stop.

Then he named the six stages of the life cycle, in a way which firmly established his Operational Product Life Cycle (see Table 8.2). These were:

1. *Primary diffusion*. The initial group of contractors and developers to whom the crane was to be offered.
2. *Penetration of all markets*. Coverage of all potential outlets.
3. *Maximum sales*.
4. *Sales decline*.
5. *Modification and reinsertion*. The possible minor changes in specification or packaging so as to reinsert the product into the life cycle curve at the point where decline has started, and to give it new life for a period.
6. *Elimination and substitution*. The point at which the market share level demands that the product be dropped and substituted by a new one.

Having established the ten action stages, Joe then began to apply some figures (either forecasts or break-even quantities) to each stage, so as to arrive at a profit figure – in other words to put some flesh on the bones of the theory. To do this he created the vertical axis of the spreadsheet, starting with:

■ total market potential (units);
■ total market potential (value);
■ company share of potential units (percentage) (see section on 'market share' calculations on p. 100);
■ company sales (units);

leading to the first major item:

■ company sales (value);

then:

- production cost of units sold;
- marketing and distribution costs;

giving:

- total costs.

This could then produce a crude contribution figure:

- difference = value minus costs;
- cumulative result;

and he added on the bottom line a figure for the time period – some estimate of how long it was expected that action stage might last.

The first point to note is that there is a clear cost incurred at each of the first four stages, and it arises not only in marketing but also in the build-up of stock for the launch. Secondly, the break-even point in terms of contribution is not reached until stage 7 (maximum sales).

Thirdly, forecasts are based on the expectation that by Stage 7, Constructa SpA will achieve a market share in units of 15 per cent. Fourthly, the process of putting the figures into the table forces all those involved to make accurate estimates of what is likely to occur at each stage. Fifth, the times shown were also estimates based on past experience and the time it might take to produce a new product.

In practice the figures that were mostly wrong were the time period ones. The launch time was twice as long, the primary diffusion much quicker than forecast and sales decline slower.

Table 8.2 *Operative Product Life Cycle for Constructa SpA*

Thousands

	SEARCH & SCREENING OF IDEAS 1	TECHNICAL MARKETING DEVELOPMENT 2	PERFORMANCE MARKETING TESTING 3	LAUNCH IN MARKET 4	PRIMARY DIFFUSION 5	PENETRATION ALL MARKETS 6	MAXIMUM SALES 7	SALES DECLINE 8	MODIFICATION REINSERTION 9	ELIMINATION SUBSTITUTION 10
TOTAL UNITS MARKET POTENTIAL	5.0	5.0	5.0	5.0	5.5	5.5	6.0	6.0	6.0	6.0
TOTAL VALUE MARKET POTENTIAL	10.0	10.0	10.0	10.0	11.0	11.0	12.0	12.0	12.0	12.0
COMPANY % SHARE UNITS POTENTIAL	–	–	–	2%	5%	10%	15%	8%	10.0	5%
COMPANY UNIT SALES	–	–	–	10	275	550	750	480	600	120
VALUE COMPANY SALES	–	–	–	22.0	605.0	1210.0	1650.0	1056.0	1320.0	264.0
PRODUCTION COST UNITS SOLD	20.0	20.0	110.0	15.0	602.5	907.5*	1237.5	871.2*	1089.0	217.8
MARKETING & DISTRIBUTION COSTS	10.0	10.0	20.0	16.0	22.75	40.5	42.5	39.8	41.0	16.2
GENERAL OVERHEAD OTHER COSTS	–	–	–	0.2	0.55	1.1	1.5	0.96	1.2	0.24
TOTAL COSTS	30.0	30.0	130.0	31.2	825.80	949.1	1281.5	911.96	1131.2	235.24
DIFFERENCE VALUE MINUS COSTS	–30	–30	–130	–9.2	–220.8	260.9	368.5	144.0	188.8	20.26
CUMULATIVE RESULT	–30.0	–60.0	–190.0	–199.2	–420.0	–159.1	209.4	353.4	542.2	570.46
TIME PERIOD (MONTHS)	3	6	3	6	6	12	12	12	6	12

*Cost variation of 10%

Market share

This case demonstrates the point that in looking at market share it is important to identify to which market the share refers. For many products there are at least four market shares which might be looked at:

■ Volume (number of units sold).
■ Value (total value of sales).
■ Number of outlets carrying the product.
■ Number of potential users who specify.

EXAMPLE

In the pharmaceutical business, Simon Majaro points out, there are a number of types of market share:

■ Number of patients with the condition.
■ Number of doctors prescribing.
■ Total number of doctors who could prescribe.
■ Number of pharmacies carrying the product.
■ Total volume of product used.

Accurate identification is essential if marketing efforts are to be directed accurately.

9

Managing the Brand

So far in this book I have used the idea of the Product Manager to include the Brand Manager. In many companies their responsibilities are the same. But there are sometimes cases where the Brand Manager has a different type of responsibility, largely because he is managing an intangible.

DEFINING THE BRAND

There seem, in general, to be three ways in which a 'brand' is defined.

- It can be the brand name attached to a product which has many competitors, in order to demonstrate, for example, that HK Kellogg or Henry Ford produced it – as distinct from some other producer of cornflakes or cars. This was, perhaps, the earliest use of 'branding' in the marketing area. Assay marks, makers' stamps and artists' names have been around for centuries. Today, however, the 'brand', in the sense shown on cornflakes or cars, is on display to the world (you cannot avoid noticing Calvin Klein T-shirts).
- A definition might be: 'a name, term, sign, symbol or design intended to differentiate goods or services.' It can be, or become, the name of an unique product – the Mars bar, the Hoover or Aspirin – which has expanded into a generic term.
- There is also a definition which subsumes the other two, suggesting that branding can be 'a concept or idea or image created in the mind of the purchaser or user'. (Penguin Books,

Marks & Spencer and Walt Disney are examples; so are the franchising of services such as Holiday Inn, McDonalds, Kall-Kwik or Spar.)

STRATEGIES AND ESSENTIALS

It is interesting for the Brand Manager to realise that there are three evident strategies which he might follow, or have to extend: one which brands an individual product (or product range), another which provides a 'brand umbrella' over the whole activity of the business (eg Nestlé), and a third which combines the two (eg Marks & Spencer and St Michael). Those who look for theories summing up current practice insist that the brand must have a concrete existence, something which can be purchased, and used or experienced. This needs to be taken into account when considering brand strategy.

Additionally there are four *essentials* of a 'Brand' which need also to be considered:

■ *first*, the aspects which distinguish the branded product/service from other products or services, such as a specific colour or shape (eg Ford's or Kellogg's hand-written signatures, KLM's logo, IKEA's name);
■ *second*, the brand must demonstrate that it provides specific benefits for particular needs (*Lemsip* and *Ribena* come to mind). But culture differences can intrude when the product enters the global market-place: (*Ovaltine* was sold in the UK as a 'last-thing-at-night' drink; while *Ovomaltine*, its continental twin, was sold as a breakfast 'pick-me-up' in other European markets);
■ *third*, the ability of the 'branding process' to be communicated to the purchaser and user (eg the current design and colours of petrol filling stations, and railway rolling-stock);
■ *fourth*, the communicated features are standardized, particularly where they appear in different markets across the world (particularly important, say, for airlines like KLM whose logo and blue colour have remained standard for more than thirty years. But, at the same time, note the change of shape of the Nescafé *Gold Blend* jar – presumably the Brand Manager assumed that the story line in the ads, and the sound of the name, were more important than the shape of the supermarket jar).

DEVISING A BRAND STRATEGY

The function description of a Product Manager in the 'fast moving consumer goods (fmcg)' field outlined in Chapter 2 suggests that his objective is: 'to maximise the contribution of Brand X to the Company's profit'. This is fine where the brand is an individual product (or product line): Heinz Soup, Heinz Baked Beans, or Heinz Alphabet Spaghetti is a good example. Indeed, it could be argued that each product should be managed by a separate Product Manager under the general supervision of a Manager of the Brand. Such a manager would need to establish objectives in *financial terms* for the brand, perhaps Return on Assets Managed [ROAM] – he will find that supermarket chains will be continuously interested in *market share* information in order to decide the amount of shelf space needed to be given to each competing product – or in *quality level terms*.

Such a Brand Manager (and his superiors) will be chiefly concerned with maintaining consumer interest in the product. The manager needs not only to 'add value' but also to entertain the shopper. Point of Purchase (POP) displays are being created which, by means of colour, interaction with shoppers or tactile display features, draw the customer towards the brand on the supermarket shelf. Merchandising – as in tasting, smelling, and touching – can help the customer/user to make decisions about brands. This means that part of the Brand Manager's armoury must be a detailed knowledge of sales promotion techniques, so that he can discuss them with Advertising Agents and supermarket Purchasing Managers.

The problem of devising a Brand Strategy becomes even more difficult when a major player (eg Nestlé) takes over another brand (eg Rowntree) and must decide whether the old brand (eg *Smarties*) is stronger than the new one (Nestlé). In some cases the original brand is retained in its strongest market, for example the *Maison du Café* brand of coffee is retained by Douwe Egbert in France, whereas Douwe Egbert have attacked the British market head-on with their Douwe Egbert's coffee. Similarly, *After Eight* has retained its brand without being identified either with its originator, Rowntree, or with its current owner, Nestlé. (It is important to bear in mind that today's examples can quickly become outdated. The whole market may well be changed by 2005 and brands are often the most ephemeral aspect of the product type – see Chapter 8 on the Product Life Cycle).

A strategy where the brand is an umbrella for all the products of the company needs to be outlined at the highest level. The 'image' presented needs consistent support, and the strategists of all the products under the umbrella must be given clear terms of reference to fit in with the brand objective of the umbrella. However, one must note the dangers for an umbrella brand, in particular the effect when one product is attacked: the attack tends to spill over to all the others. (The Nestlé umbrella suffered from those who disapproved of its policy of selling powdered milk in Africa, while Shell's petrol stations suffered when it proposed to dump a redundant North Sea platform into the North Atlantic.)

There have fairly recently been some tidying up activities in the UK by major global brands. 'Mullard', owned by Philips since 1928, became 'Philips Components' sixty years later. The pharmaceutical company 'May & Baker', which had been bought by Rhône Poulenc in the twenties, became 'Rhône Poulenc Pharmaceuticals' in the late eighties. Both moves can be seen to be designed to meet the challenge of globalization.

STRATEGIC CHOICES

Individual brands, like individual products, face a number of strategic choices; since it is the brand which, to coin a phrase, is branded by the customer/ user/ consumer with a position in the market place, the Brand Manager needs to make a choice - and follow it through.

First, to answer a number of questions.

1. Should the brand demonstrate better quality at a higher price *or* the same quality at lower price?
2. Should the offer be a 'head-on' one – ie the same as the competition, but better – or one that aims at the 'blind side' of an unoccupied niche market?
3. Are we managing a large brand in a mass market, *or* a low volume/high profit brand in a speciality market?

These questions can only be answered for an existing Brand by detailed market research (as discussed in Chapter 3), with all the caveats mentioned in that chapter! The problems of developing a new brand are tackled in Chapter 10.

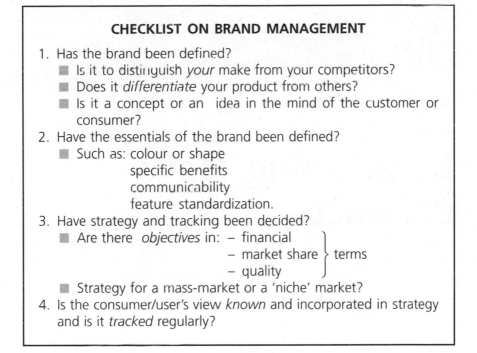

CHECKLIST ON BRAND MANAGEMENT

1. Has the brand been defined?
   - ■ Is it to distinguish *your* make from your competitors?
   - ■ Does it *differentiate* your product from others?
   - ■ Is it a concept or an idea in the mind of the customer or consumer?
2. Have the essentials of the brand been defined?
   - ■ Such as: colour or shape
     specific benefits
     communicability
     feature standardization.
3. Have strategy and tracking been decided?
   - ■ Are there *objectives* in: – financial
     – market share } terms
     – quality
   - ■ Strategy for a mass-market or a 'niche' market?
4. Is the consumer/user's view *known* and incorporated in strategy and is it *tracked* regularly?

10

Developing New Products

ROUTES TO GROWTH

One of the major pressures on the product manager is the need for growth. She needs first to examine the possible routes to growth to see which provides a balance tilted in its favour. Here are five possible routes with their pros and cons.

Revitalisation of existing products

As we shall see, for most product managers this is the only option and in its favour is the fact that it exploits existing assets (such as brand image, satisfied customers, company knowledge and expertise). Against it is the fact that too many products are kept in the range which ought to have been discontinued; the costs of revitalisation may not be repaid and the product may die anyway.

Developing foreign markets

One of the great successes of global brands is their identification of similar market segments in many different countries. Many businesses, with considerable benefit, can expand into foreign markets (even with technology that is not absolutely the latest, hottest, just-off-the-drawing-board!). However, the danger is that if this route is followed it may well be treated too casually by other important managers within the business.

Joint ventures

This route would include 'co-makership' or joining with a producer of complementary products or services to utilise the synergy of a joint venture. It can lead to a quick contribution to profits but arguments can arise easily as to the ratio of shared profits going to each party.

Acquisition

The route of acquiring either a competitive product or a complementary business could certainly lead to a considerable increase in revenue and possibly a boost to market share. However, acquisitions always bring with them the likelihood of underestimation of the risks involved. Often the acquisition looks good on paper but when the strengths and weaknesses of the acquired business are looked at more thoroughly in terms of staff and systems, frequently a more dangerous aspect is revealed.

New Product Development (NPD)

As a route to growth NPD has in its favour the fact that it uses the company's strengths; the business develops new products which arise from its own expertise; it puts its efforts into them; it owns them. Against this route is both its risk and its cost. Business literature is littered with stories of immensely expensive failures; and some quite cheap successes. Both cost and risk need careful assessment in advance.

THE PROFIT GAP

The drive towards new product development may also be fuelled by the existence of a gap between what is needed to maintain the continuity of the business and what is feasible with existing products. Current expectations can demonstrate quite a large gap between what is desired and what is realistic. This can show itself as a profit gap (see Figure 10.1).

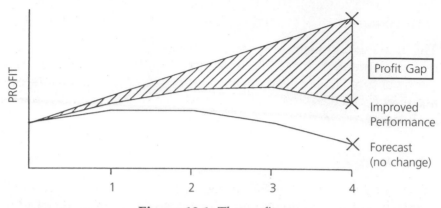

Figure 10.1 *The profit gap*

The Ansoff matrix (Figure 10.2) gives a starting-point for filling the gaps.

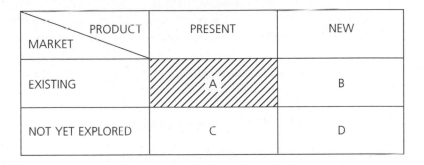

Figure 10.2 *Ansoff's matrix*

For each of the boxes in Figure 10.2 it is important for the product manager to estimate how much of the profit gap it can fill.

		Value	*%*
(A) = market penetration – *present* products in *present* markets, increased market share.		€xxx	y
(B) = product development – *new* products in *present* markets.		€xxx	y
(C) = market development – *present* products in *new* markets.		€xxx	y
(D) = diversification – *new* products in *new* markets.		€xxx	y
	Total	€xxx	
	Profit gap	€xxx	
	Balance	?	

RESTRICTIONS FOR EXISTING PRODUCT MANAGERS

It is often the case that the product or brand manager with an existing brand is limited in what she can accomplish in new product development. Organisationally she is restricted to:

■ Reformulating the product – and that within fairly narrow limits – which might give it additional attributes.

■ Manipulating the price in some way to make the product *look* different to present customers.
■ Changing the packaging – but in such a way as not to damage the brand's identity or market standing.
■ Increasing expenditure on sales promotion, advertising or selling.
■ Rethinking communication strategy and the content of promotion.

But if one can undertake new product development then all elements are variable and all the company's strengths can and should be utilised. Therefore, new product development needs to be examined from the following points of view:

■ organisation;
■ a systematic approach to creativity and development;
■ development stages plus screening and testing.

ORGANISING NEW PRODUCT DEVELOPMENT

More than a flow of new and brilliant ideas we need the machinery to ensure that these ideas are carried through. The Sappho project, which studied the success and failure of industrial innovation, came to some universal conclusions having studied more than 70 case histories of innovations. It concluded that firms were most successful in innovating stressed marketing; and that successful innovating firms:

■ understand user end requirements better;
■ employ greater sales efforts;
■ make greater efforts to educate users;
■ give more publicity to innovation.

Other success characteristics included:

■ seeking the innovation deliberately and not relying on chance;
■ employing larger project teams than competitors;
■ being less divided internally about the commercial prospects of the innovation.

Experience shows that there are four major organisational forms which can run new product development:

1. An NPD product planner – someone who is part of the product management group, reporting to a group product manager.
2. Extending the product (brand) manager's responsibilities to cover new product development.
3. A product development committee.
4. A new product development division or department which takes on the whole function, including launching the product and managing it for 12 months before handing it over to an existing product manager.

Whichever form is chosen for new product development it must fulfil the following criteria:

▪ should meet objectives in terms of profitable new products;
▪ should co-exist and co-operate with the rest of the company without friction and inefficiencies;
▪ should avoid excessive investment in failures and abandoned products;
▪ should have a sufficient workload to justify its existence.

The principles on which it operates should be as follows:

▪ its function should be separate;
▪ if a committee, it should be fully representative of operating departments;
▪ it should be responsible for:
  – seeking for ideas/sources of ideas;
  – evaluating ideas;
  – screening projects;
  – maintaining control documents;
  – co-ordinating progress.

The need for careful consideration of the organisation of new product development is evident from the following quotation (from Joe Cagnina, again, in a lecture to Management Centre Europe).

EXAMPLE

Various studies furnish ample evidence that all too often:

■ programmes are undertaken without sufficient market data;
■ products are developed and go into production without direct reference to the buyer or consumer ... or testing;
■ sales and promotional commitments are made without test-marketing experience;
■ marketing management's role and attitude is administrative and 'protective' rather than dynamic and innovative.

The results are an unduly high number of unsuccessful launchings, pressure withdrawals before pay-off, low-level sales and profit performance ... or over-age products showing evident symptoms of forthcoming collapse.

On the other hand there are countless examples of products which did not exist five or ten years ago but have conquered dominant market positions in a short time. Their success may be traced directly to clear product conception, imaginative design, careful testing, aggressive promotion and continuous control complemented by objective evaluations: all evidence of methodical planning and dynamic marketing management.

Many other companies can also boast of middle-aged products which are just as profitably vigorous as when first introduced, clearly demonstrating that innovation does not always depend on absolute 'novelty'.

The advantages of a single manager, whether the product manager or a new product development manager, over a committee are that:

■ one person has a major concern for the product line;
■ action taken will be customer-oriented;
■ functional responsibilities remain intact;
■ day-to-day activities can be separated.

On the other hand experience with a well-functioning product policy committee shows that it can co-ordinate conflicting views and ensure that all those responsible are kept up to date. Indeed it may often be worthwhile for the product manager to act as secretary/administrator to the committee.

Two documents are basic essentials which apply throughout the new product development process:

1. *Idea information record,* which can control the process right through (see Table 10.3).
2. *Technical and market newness responsibility chart,* which identifies the current developments in a company and specifies action and responsibility (see Table 10.4). This is an extension of the Ansoff matrix (Figure 10.2).

EXAMPLE

New product strategy – 'opportunity cost and development risk' – a general theory by Charles Jones of McKinsey.

These two major considerations influence the decisions as to the length of time (and hence the resource application) development should take.

If opportunity costs are *high* due to the current risks of loss of volume or market share, loss of key customers, loss of control over distribution or loss of sustainable advantage – your product is no longer the standard – then you should concentrate on a short development time, so as to claw back market leadership.

If opportunity costs are *low* because future demand or value to the customer are uncertain, or because the technologies are leading-edge rather than state-of-the-art, or perhaps technologies are being combined, or there is no guideline as to the breadth of the product line. In these cases a longer development time is advised.

An example of each:

■ IBM PC – became a necessity because the current loss of market share created an opportunity cost of over $1 billion. The project which would normally have taken four years was completed in 15 months.

■ Boeing 767 – opportunity cost was low because no such plane existed but the development risks, financial and technical, were high: new aircraft costing upwards of $1.5 billion. Boeing embarked on a programme to get it 100 per cent right with extensive testing and intensive involvement with the initial customer, there being major new technological and technical innovations.

Table 10.3 *Idea information record*

Product development screening committee

Idea information record

No:
Date of origin:
Minute no:

New/improved product

Stage I. Idea investigation

Title — Product division

Brief description:

By whom sponsored: — When:

Initial consideration by committee

Market acceptability:	Manufacture practicability:
Profitability:	Engineering practicability:
Research feasibility:	Merchandising suitability:
Material supply:	No established competitive similarity:

(Mark: 'X' – probable; 'Y' – possible; 'Z' – doubtful)

Decided second stage investigation / /

Decided to reject — Committee secretary

Stage II. Idea investigation

Comments by:

Divisional sales manager

Costing executive

Divisional production manager

Process engineer

Material supplies executive

Marketing manager

Committee's recommendation: reject/shelve project

Sponsor informed and given reasons for recommendation / /

If projected, priority: deferred/normal/top

Project no.

Top management decision:

Reject/shelve project — Committee secretary

Priority: deferred/normal/top — Managing director

Table 10.4 *Classification of sales and technical development*

Note:
The reference letters for current development projects listed have been used here to illustrate the classification of projects by technical and market newness and the corresponding areas of responsibility

	Increasing technical newness: manufacturing managers responsible →		
Increasing market newness: general sales manager responsible ↓	No technical change. No technical research work necessary	Development in the use of your present manufacturing skill and raw materials. Requires research into existing methods	New manufacturing skills to be acquired. Requires research into new materials and new production techniques
No market change. Sales programme unaffected	*(Present business)*	*Revise manufacturing methods*	*Seek better manufacturing processes* R
Better share of existing market to be obtained. Requires expansion of your sales programme	*Increase market coverage and . . .*	*. . . make existing products more widely acceptable in the present market* C H K L N P S	*Extend the existing product range* A D E G Q T U
New markets to be entered. Requires investigation into new markets and selling techniques	*Seek new uses for existing products*	*Modify the products to suit new markets* B J M O	*Develop new processes to make new products for new markets* F I

PRODUCT CHARACTERISTICS

Before going further, product managers should check the following questionnaire about product characteristics and tick as appropriate:

Do your customers *appreciate*:

☐ New convenience in use (power steering, recharge of copier cartridges, lap tops)?
☐ New performance (faster, easier, biological washing powder, computer-aided mapping, video recording)?
☐ New availability (snack trolleys on trains, 'flying' pizzas, hot food at filling stations)?
☐ Status symbols (health clubs, home Jacuzzis)?
☐ Credibility of benefits (health foods and pills, make-up)?
☐ New cost or price?

Do they *dislike*:

☐ New method of use (complicated instrument panels)?
☐ Unfamiliar pattern of use (zappers, Internet)?
☐ Unfamiliar benefit ('it is genuinely designed to rationalise your multiple servers into one as your network burgeons')?
☐ Costliness of error in use (wiping of computer program)?

Do they *worry* about:

☐ New appearance (ghetto blaster)?
☐ Different kind of service (home tuning of cars)?
☐ New sales channels (videos from a filling station)?

A SYSTEMATIC APPROACH TO NEW PRODUCT DEVELOPMENT

It is often said that creativity is needed in the development of new products and that creativity cannot be turned on and off like a tap. Here is a technique which *can* allow a systematic approach to creativity and development in five major steps.

1. situation analysis;
2. objective setting;

3. assessing possibilities;
4. selecting the best potential;
5. development plans.

Situation analysis

The situation to be analysed is 'the need for a new product'. The first step is to assemble as wide a collection of facts as possible on the following basis:

■ *What* problems need to be solved?
  – A customer requirement?
  – A fault in an existing product?
  – The decline of present products?
  – Competitive action leading to reduced market share?
■ *Who* is currently involved in the problem?
  – What market segment needs the new product?
  – Which group of salesmen or customers?
  – What competitors have caused trouble?
  – Which manufacturing techniques?
■ *Where* has the need arisen?
  – Is this a true problem to be solved?
  – Is it in a particular geographical area?
  – Is it volume or profit?
■ Since *when* has it been a noticeable problem?
  – At what stage of the existing product life cycle is it proposed to insert a new product? (*See Chapter 8*)

Only when facts have been collected, can opinions be sought as to why the problems have arisen, whether innovation is the answer or whether there are simpler solutions. The 'whys' can lead to the setting of priorities in the next stage.

Objective setting and establishing criteria

As with any decision-making process or problem-solving technique, the essential next step is to establish the parameters of the solution, in terms of the objectives being aimed at and the criteria of acceptability. The objectives the solution must achieve, for example:

■ it must meet certain customer needs;
■ it must solve the identified customer problem;

- the product (new or modified) must have certain specific attributes;
- its relationship with existing products must fit a specified pattern;
- it must be aimed at a particular market segment;
- it must fall within given price and cost parameters;
- it must be launched within a given time (see 'new product strategy theory' above) and within an investment level.

Develop alternatives

At this stage what is needed is a number of ideas from which to choose those which might satisfy the criteria. Figure 10.3 presents a synoptic view of how the product manager or the new product development committee can search for ideas for new products or service. Reading clockwise from the top left of the figure the product manager can choose from ten sources of ideas – or can use all ten!

Figure 10.3 *Location of ideas*

Market research
For the purposes of new product ideas, research should be aimed at areas of consumer dissatisfaction. What do consumers find difficult to understand or to handle? David Blunkett, the Minister for Education and Employment, in a recent letter to *The Times* wrote:

> If the consumer is dissatisfied with the product it is the producer and not the user who is at fault! Too often these days you are made to feel that there is something slightly strange and old-fashioned about you if you don't like the over-sophistication of products which make the job in hand take longer and the learning process more complicated.

Too often market research is used as a prop for advertising and sales promotion.

Long range planning studies
One of the major influences on product acceptability or otherwise is the change occurring in economic wellbeing and the relaxation in social constraints. Examining these can help indicate directions in new product development.

Market gap analysis
A careful examination of the range of existing products on offer to users may well reveal gaps in the market – in (say) sizes, types, prices, features – which might be filled to advantage. (One of the most famous gaps was identified by BMW when it first put on the road an executive saloon car which catered for the executive who wanted a car with the liveliness of a sports car but the appearance of a business vehicle.)

Think tank
In recent years a number of political think tanks have been set up to provide party politicians with new ideas. A commercial think tank set up with people who have broad experience and an unbiased approach can help to explore the effects of a changing society on consumer needs and can identify, perhaps, potentially profitable niches in a future market.

Activity analysis
I have argued elsewhere in this book that product managers should take into account the way in which products and services are actually used. Careful analysis of consumption systems can not only

help to identify changes needed in promotional activity or distribution systems but can highlight new product opportunities.

Foreign search
Someone recently remarked at a conference: 'Marketing doesn't stop at Dover'. The way in which problems have been solved in countries outside the UK is always worth examining (and not just to reinforce our insularity). This is true in all kinds of different aspects of life, from the construction of motorways to the operation of banking services.

Translation of foreign experience
We may recognise that a solution to a problem in another country is superior but it may be necessary to think very carefully about translating foreign experience into a product or service offered in the UK. (For example, the company which gave its UK-manufactured product a Japanese name; the company which manufactured cars in Malaysia with Japanese technology; Italian ice-cream manufactured in the UK; Italian sauce manufactured in Holland!).

Design factor analysis
Pre-Raphaelites, Art Deco, 1930s nostalgia, phallic symbolism, naked ladies – all types of design base which attract or repel customers/ users by provoking a response to the image presented (see Chapter 4). Of course image response is much more sophisticated than that but the identification of image response can often make the difference between success and failure. (Bring in your advertising agency – see 'the advertising brief' in Chapter 7.)

Brainstorming and other creativity techniques
Brainstorming is the best known technique, where no criticism is offered and the search is for the greatest possible number of ideas (see boxed text on page 121).

Synectics, a more disciplined approach to group creativity, which tries to develop states of mind using personal analogies (what would *you* do if *you* were a . . . ?), direct analogies (biological, mechanical, natural solutions) and symbolic analogies for crucial or unclear parts of the problem (words, pictures, images from other media).

Morphological analysis is a method which can take the different dimensions of a problem and explore them separately (eg the appearance of a watch face as being quite separate from its mechanism, its accuracy or its mount) or it can be used in matrix form, suggesting the ways in which one axis can influence the other.

Lateral thinking, invented by Edward de Bono, attempts to get participants to break out of their 'mind-set' and to search for different ways of looking at things.

EXAMPLE

Note on brainstorming technique

Step 1. Prior selection of the *problem*.
Step 2. Selection of the *group* (10–12 people).
Step 3. *Duration:*
    – simple problems: 30 minutes;
    – normal problems: one hour;
    – special problems: one hour 30 minutes.
Step 4. *Implementation:*
    – statement of the problem;
    – brainstorming rules: suspended judgment, free-wheeling welcomed, quantity encouraged, cross-fertilisation;
    – evaluation: selection criteria put forward, two or three ideas selected for further processing;
    – reverse (negative) brainstorming: in how many ways can selected ideas fall?
Step 5. *Proposal.*

Technological ideas breakthrough

This, the conventional source, is your own research or development department. There is, however, a strong temptation to consider that its members spend all their time researching uncommercial problems!

This whole exercise should result in a list of possible products or product modification.

Identify possible resultant snags

From the alternatives it is now feasible to do two things:

1. Identify the kind of problems which may arise:
   – the product will not work;
   – the cost is too high;
   – marketing effort is too expensive;
   – channels of distribution will not play.

2. Create a couple of screens through which the new idea/product must pass.

The screening process

1. Assess the company's resources needed to develop and launch the product on the market:

■ sufficient finance available for risk taking;
■ access to raw material;
■ need for new plant or premises;
■ plant expansion possible/desirable;
■ patent situation, licensing possibility, franchising;
■ relevance of public image;
■ past experience in this product/market area;
■ skilled manufacturing/selling/operating/service staff;
■ management skills needed.

2. Table 10.5 shows a screen which attempts to cover all the marketing aspects of a new product or service. Taking one product or service, respondents (or the committee) are asked to weight the importance to them of each opportunity/constraint and then to rate the product or service on a zero to ten scale as to its fit with the company. Multiplying the weighting and the rating gives a score in the last column. This is a starting-point for discussion as to the acceptability of the proposed new product into the company's range.

EXAMPLE: DEVELOPING A NEW BRAND

a) Select an agreed brand name
b) Select an agreed entry strategy from the following suggestions:
   1) deliberate search for markets unlikely to attract heavy spenders (such as detergents, food, drinks etc);
   2) seek control over distribution outlets (direct, via selected wholesalers);
   3) choose direct selling - 'off the page' (in magazines), via 'free' telephone numbers;
   4) seek markets outside core areas (such as garage forecourt shops);

> 5) look for possible brand expansion, ie attaching the brand name to other 'unconnected' products (perhaps, After Eight to silk underwear, or perfume?).
> c) Ensure the 'product' or 'service' works - and is right for the chosen consumer.
> d) Prepare the launch: – sales promotion;
>   – advertising;
>   – pricing;
>   – distributor's margin;
>   – planned dates.
> e) Establish objectives and set up controls for test marketing.
> f) Check results.
> g) 'All systems go!' (or STOP).

TESTING, TEST MARKETING AND LAUNCHING

The final stage of a systematic approach is to list action requirements under the following headings:

■ Steps to be taken (in logical order).
■ By whom (individuals and groups).
■ Time limits and deadlines for the steps.
■ Control system (review and update).
■ What happens if . . . (it fails, it is late, it is wrong)?

So development of the product proceeds under careful, regular control until the time comes for it to be tested. First there are performance tests:

1. For industrial products:
   – performance: to check that the product actually does what it is planned to do, that its specification is correct;
   – durability: that it will stand up to the most severe treatment it is designed to withstand;
   – output and efficiency: whether the ratios of input to output are as planned.
2. For consumer products, tests to ensure that they fit consumer requirements as far as:
   – formulation: it is in line with local and international regulations;
   – taste;

Table 10.5 Products ideas screening

Opportunity or constraint	(Max 20) Weight A	Fit with company 0–10		(Max 10) Rating B	Score A × B
		Low (0)	**High (10)**		
Selling		New organisation needed	Fits existing salesforce		
Marketing		New market to be approached	Appeals to existing market		
Competition		Entrenched and strong	Ample unfilled demand		
Company image		Diminishes it	Major boost		
Reputation in same field		None	Dominant		
Product's attributes		Very complicated and difficult	Simple and straightforward		
Packaging		Complete repacking needed	No change needed		
Supply		Unreliable in unsuitable quantities	Regular in right quantities		
Purchase		New field	Knowledge and contacts		
Distribution		More space needed. Different transport needs	Use present warehouse and transport		
Distribution channels		New channel	Present channels		
Profitability		Below average	High volume and margin		
Personnel		New staff needed	Present staff can cope		

- touch;
- shape;
- packaging: efficient both in appearance and protection.

EXAMPLE

Industrial trade and consumer associations usually have set up technical performance tests for cars, textiles, machines, detergents, chemicals and electronics – mostly to fit BSI standards.

Consumer acceptance tests are also set up by market research agencies and may include:

■ use of the company's own personnel (for the sake of security) to give a view of the product;
■ trying out on a random sample of the population selected on the same basis as a market research sample;
■ using focus groups including the company's development managers and technicians to discuss actual usage patterns;
■ for consumer durables, placement tests and loan of equipment for trial purposes;
■ selection and use of a controlled test market – usually a defined area with its own commercial television stations to enable a controlled experiment to be made.

The information which should be obtained should cover not only the acceptability (or otherwise) of the product but also:

■ the salesforce's ability to sell it;
■ the quality of the distribution channels;
■ the price level of the product;
■ the profitability, discount structures and margins;
■ market share expectations;
■ likely repurchase rate (first purchases are often test purchases);
■ how effective the marketing mix has been – is the balance of factors right?

Now, the evaluation of the success or otherwise of the test market. The product manager should create a checklist – if the evaluation is favourable – for the launch (and a checklist only asks the questions; it does not answer them).

CHECKLIST

Here is a checklist about a checklist!

■ Does your checklist for the launch of the new product take into account:
  - who the potential user is ⎫ on whom the success of the
  - who the decision maker is ⎭ product depends?
■ Does the checklist contain careful costings – including the over-heads with which you are likely to be landed?
■ Have you established results expected – month by month, quarter by quarter?
■ Have you covered the advertising and promotion programmes?
■ What about after-sales service?
■ What about communication with sales and service personnel?
■ What about physical distribution?
■ What about the distributors? Do you know them? Do they like you?
■ Have you taken into account the effect on other products/services?

11

Control and Communication

RETURN ON INVESTMENT (ROI)

The product manager needs to understand (indeed to be familiar with) the return on investment (ROI) formula. It was devised originally so as to arrive at an effective and valid measurement of the return achieved on an investment no matter what type of disparate businesses, products or services were to be compared. The formula is shown as Figure 11.1.

This formula can be used for a number of purposes, eg:

- comparison of one year's results with another;
- noting a trend over five years;
- comparing one division of a company or one product with another;
- setting targets for each unit or subsidiary;
- identifying the influence of the building blocks.

It is in the last that the formula can perhaps best be used by product managers.

As can be seen from Figure 11.1 the ROI can be divided into percentage profit on sales (return on sales) and the rate of asset turnover (sales divided by total assets or capital employed), which means that a low return on capital employed can be due either to falling profit margins or to a low rate of asset turnover, or both! [The best illustration of the formula lies in the comparison between

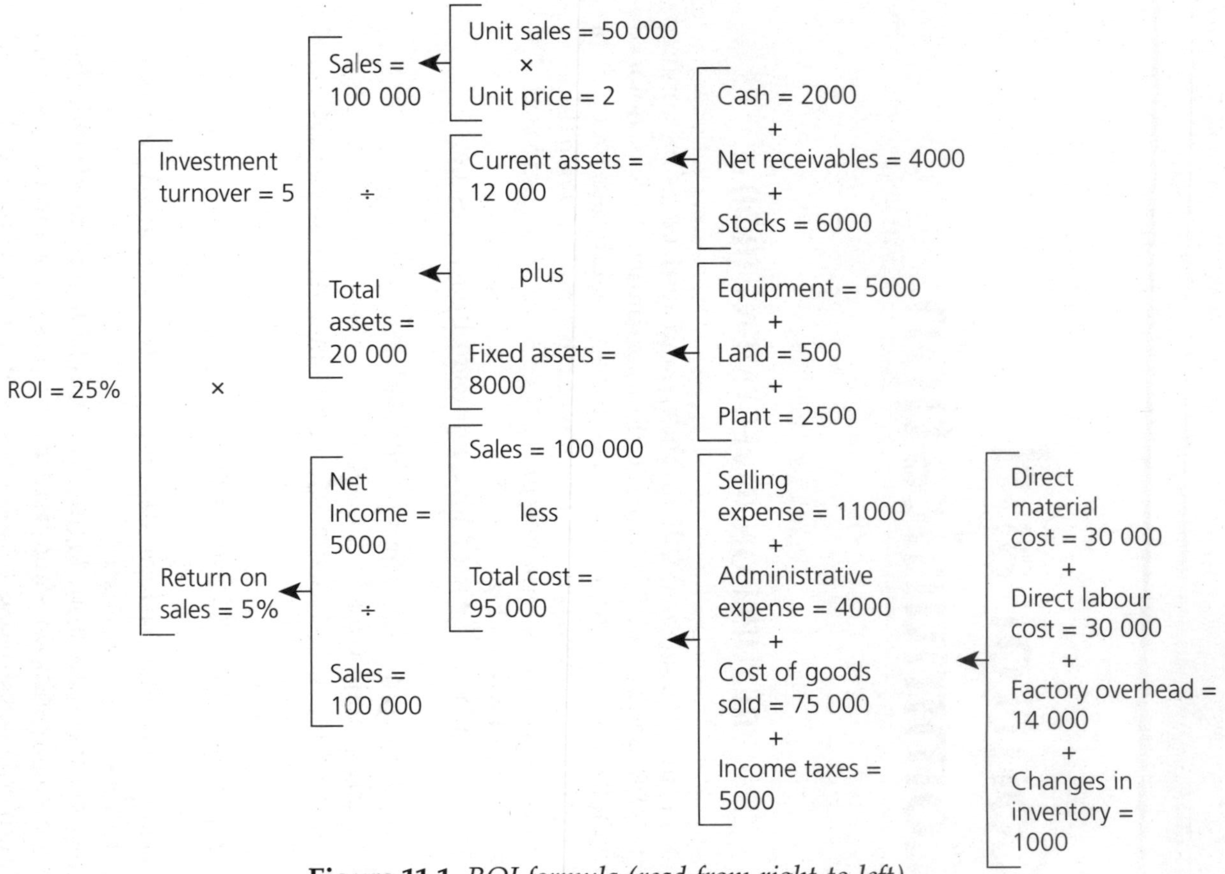

Figure 11.1 *ROI formula (read from right to left)*

a department store and a supermarket, each of which had an ROI of 20 per cent. The supermarket achieved this by a turnover of assets of ten times per year and a profit margin of 2 per cent. The department store had an asset turnover of two times per year and a profit margin of 10 per cent.]

Apart from external comparisons or those for the separate divisions or units within the company, calculations can be made of the return on assets managed (ROAM) for each product. This assumes that, at the budgeting stage, the different building blocks can be apportioned fairly without too much argument or frustration.

EVALUATING INVESTMENT

Cash flows

For investing in the development of new products it is also important to forecast the flow of cash (both negative and positive) so as to argue whether the product is, of itself, a good use of the company's money. For this purpose three aspects need to be looked at:

1. what capital is employed in existing product groups;
2. what capital is invested in new products;
3. how such investment can be evaluated.

The capital employed in a business can be divided into:

■ fixed assets;
■ working capital (or circulating capital) which is equal to current assets (stocks, cash and easily negotiable securities and debtors) less current liabilities (creditors, dividends, etc).

The dynamic aspects of cash are shown in Figure 11.2, which also shows the relationship between fixed and working capital. This demonstrates that in the trading cycle cash flows via creditors into raw materials, work in progress and finished stocks and thence into debtors. Profit created by trading comes into the cash pool via debtors. Fixed assets and longer-term liabilities are difficult to alter quickly or in the short term. However, it is possible to affect the cash situation by manipulating the variables.

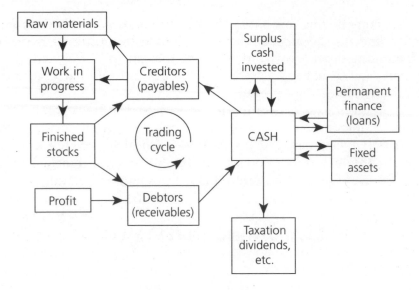

Figure 11.2 *Trading cycle*

Product managers can have (and are often expected to have) some influence on the cash flow. Marketing efforts with an existing product can mean increased coverage of the market; to cope with this there would need to be increased cash tied up in receivables as well as in finished stocks, in order to cover increased expectations. A shortage of cash can imply action in the form of quicker collection of receivables, running down stocks and reducing work in progress. Accounts departments will usually help by extending credit taken from suppliers; production departments can help by reducing the length of the production cycle.

There is usually a trade-off. Extending credit taken from suppliers can result in prompt payment discounts being lost. Running down stocks can cause sales to be lost. Pressure on debtors can cause loss of good will. Such penalties must be set off against their positive influence on cash flow.

One can take this decision process further and apply it to the ROI pattern shown earlier. For example, the launch of a new product will involve manufacturing, selling and administrative costs. The profit margin will need to cover these in order to produce a satisfactory percentage on that arm of the ROI chart. The same product launch will increase working capital by increasing stocks of all kinds, probably increasing net debtors (receivables minus payables) and possibly will have involved increasing fixed assets in the form of new machinery. If the targeted return on investment figure is to be reached, fresh calculations will need to be made all through.

Forecasts

The detailed working out of the investment in new products (or projects) and the return on that investment is usually left to those who have a liking for figures. The more creative marketing people feel themselves above such things. Even when the approach is explained there are still those who find the matter either too difficult or irrelevant to the real business. This book is not the place to give the whole detailed background of the financial analysis of a new product, the intention is to show some of the signposts *en route*.

For some services (such as consultancy), there may be less need to consider the pay-back possibilities of an investment. However, for capital intensive services the purchase of a hotel or an aircraft requires the most careful analysis on the lines shown below (specifically in Table 11.2 for 'plant' read 'hotel' or 'aircraft').

Along with the control on the development of new products outlined in Chapter 10, there is a need to create the forecasts of different aspects of the project and then to examine the assumptions behind those forecasts.

First, forecasts must be made of capacity and production required, stocks and sales turnover in units, to see whether the project will actually work. Such forecasts can be shown either on an annual scale or detailed as a series of action stages on a new product launch, eg:

■ idea search;
■ screening;
■ test marketing;
■ launch and primary diffusion;
■ total coverage/saturation;
■ decline.

The planning horizon has much to do with the product's expected life cycle as shown in Chapter 8 (see Table 8.2).

Second, to make forecasts of investment required, along with the necessary assumptions, split into buildings, machinery, etc, and the annual requirements over the length of the project's life.

Third, to make similarly charted forecasts of revenue, together with assumptions of price levels.

Fourth, to make a kind of profit and loss statement forecast for each year of the planned project's life.

From these forecasts an assumption about working capital requirement over the period must be charted.

Payback and discounted cash flow (DCF)

The product manager needs to be able to defend himself against the ways in which decisions on investment in his product may go. The principal methods of making decisions as to whether an investment is worthwhile are:

■ payback period;
■ profit on sales;
■ return on investment;
■ discounted cash flow (or present value).

Return on investment has been examined and appears to be more concerned with target setting and analysis than with future projects (though it provides a basis for discounted cash flow calculations).

Profit on sales or return on sales ratio is a good measure for annual observation but, because the level of investment is often disregarded, it is difficult to use for new projects.

The *payback method* works on the basis of the number of years it will take for a project to pay for itself out of its earnings (a method, in domestic life, used in discussion of the cost of insulation against the reduction in heating bills). By this method the project which will pay for itself in the shortest time after the date of the original investment is the winner (see Table 11.1).

Based on the payback method, project A would be preferred because its payback period is two years whereas project B's payback period is three years. The disadvantages of the system are evident here:

■ the ROI for project B is in fact higher;
■ no account is taken of profits arising after the investment has been paid for;
■ definition of profits is not clear;
■ the time value of money is ignored.

It seems essential therefore to look more closely at DCF (or present value method).

Table 11.1 *Payback calculation*

	Project A €	Project B €
Cost	10,000	10,000
Estimated future profits		
Year 1	5,000	2,000
Year 2	5,000	4,000
Year 3	2,000	4,000
Year 4	2,000	6,000

The present value method (or discounted cash flow) has as its basis the calculation of the present value of future sums of money:

▪ €100 invested at 10 per cent per annum (compound) would accumulate to €121 in two years.
▪ €121 received in two years' time has a present value of €100. Present value is thus the reverse of compound interest.

Therefore the following formula can be used:

$$P = S \times \frac{1}{(1 + r)n}$$

where:

P = present value;
S = future sum;
r = interest rate expressed as a ratio (10 per cent = 0.1);
n = number of years.

The yardstick against which a project is judged is whether the present value of cash inflows exceeds the cost of the project, when using a reasonable rate of interest, such as the alternative opportunity for investing the capital (in building societies or gilt-edged securities).

For example, to arrive at net cash inflow the items shown in Table 11.2 need to be considered over a period of (say) five years.

(*Note:* profits have been taken realistically as profits after tax. Depreciation is added back as part of the net cash inflow. Working capital includes stocks, cash and net debtors.)

Table 11.2 *Net cash inflow*

Year	1	2	3	4	5	Total
Item:	€000s					
Investment in plant, etc	(60)	(30)	–	(10)	–	(100)
Profit after tax	–	(10)	5	35	50	80
Depreciation	–	6	9	7	4	26
Working capital	–	(15)	(6)	(3)	24	–
Net cash inflow	–60	–49	8	29	78	+6

( ) = minus

Table 11.3 *Present value calculations*

Cash inflow	–60	–49	8	29	78	
12% present value factor	×0.893 = –54	×0.797 = –39	×0.712 = 6	×0.635 = 18	×0.567 = 44	Result –25
5% present value factor	×0.952 = –57	×0.907 = –44	×0.864 = 7	×0.823 = 24	×0.783 = 61	–9
2% present value factor	×0.980 = –59	×0.961 = –47	×0.942 = 8	×0.924 = 27	×0.906 = 71	= 0

Applying a present value factor as shown in the formula above to each of the net cash inflow figures, the result is as shown in Table 11.3.

This demonstrates that the rate of return on the project is 2 per cent. Doing this kind of exercise on a spreadsheet allows some further work to be done to discover what changes need to be made in the initial forecast to bring the project up to a reasonable or acceptable rate of return. (*Note:* a table of present values is a useful tool for speeding the calculation and is available on any spreadsheet package.)

CONTROL SYSTEMS

Effective management control is essential to ensure that planned results are achieved. To establish a control system the following steps are necessary:

- decide which factors should be controlled;
- decide the layout and frequency of reports;
- communicate to the personnel concerned the purpose and importance of the controls.

As shown earlier the financial factors established within the planning process would include:

- sales volume and value;
- gross contribution (margin) by market;
- marketing expenses;
- net contribution (net profit).

This could be split by territories or customers as well. The factors controlled should also include working capital (stocks, net debtors, cash) and possibly non-financial factors such as complaints, delivery statistics and sales effort.

Allocation questions

This should enable the product manager to check on the progress of her product in its market and on the cost pattern of the factors (which often are outside her control). There is a problem, however. Such a control system concentrates on already planned actions. It is only at the earlier planning stage that the really difficult questions can be asked:

- 'Would €150,000 be better spent on market research or sales promotion?'
- 'Would €300,000 be better allocated to price reduction or to improving distributors' margins?'

Comparison of the effectiveness of different inputs needs to be undertaken each year at planning time.

Inherent product appeal

If the product manager is to control marketing effectiveness there is a need to examine the relationship between the different marketing factors, and in particular to try to assess inherent product appeal.

Not all sales, in fact, are the result of selling. A large proportion of the revenue of many companies occurs because customers seek out a particular product and not as a result of selling effort. This thought leads to two further points of discussion. If there are two products or product lines which have roughly the same revenue and selling and sales promotion activity is withdrawn from both, it is extremely unlikely that sales will drop to zero even over a long period. Not only that but the amount (or proportion) of revenue lost will also vary – which will demonstrate the differing effect of the input of promotion activities on different product lines.

If, then, similar amounts of money, time and effort spent on selling and sales promotion produce differing results in terms of product line revenue, there must be a point where effort should be shifted to *improving* the product rather than *promoting* it. This point will vary from one industry or business to another but there must come a point in each product's existence when the product manager can say: 'When more than x per cent of the selling price is absorbed by persuasion costs, then something should be done to modify or improve (or scrap) the product.'

Marketing cost analysis

The product manager should also challenge the system of lumping together all marketing expenses and allocating them arbitrarily. Present systems of collecting and analysing costs are usually based on natural expense classifications, such as:

■ wages and salaries;
■ invoicing;
■ transport or advertising (see Table 11.4).

Thus the product manager can be attacked on the fact that costs are rising but has no way of establishing what has caused the rise in costs nor where those costs apply. The argument is not difficult to sustain, therefore, that the information system should enable (nay, help) a product manager to examine the cost structure per territory, product and customer. Territories would be chosen on the basis that total revenue from a territory is related to the cost of servicing it. Products might be classified by the differences in sales volume/ value. Customers might be classified in groups according to the annual value of business received.

To arrive at the contribution per territory, customer group or product line it is necessary first to identify the costs which would be saved if the company stopped selling in a particular territory, supplying a group of customers or offering certain products. The basis of allocation is shown in Table 11.4.

Table 11.4 *Basis of allocation of costs, collected under natural expense headings*

Natural expense group	Basis of allocation		
	Territories	Customers	Products
1. *Order processing* Clerical labour costs, order processing and invoicing Telephone and postage Stationery	Number of orders	Number of orders or number of items	Number of orders/invoice lines for product
2. *Selling* Salary Commission Expenses Proportion of sales manager	Direct plus (*SM* ÷ by number of salespeople)	Cost per call × average number of calls per annum on customer group	Work study so as to apportion a salesperson's time to selling each product
3. *Transport* Actual carriage costs Vehicle depreciation, expenses Insurance	Values of orders	Value of orders Number of items	Value of orders
4. *Reimbursement* (Allowance for bad debts) (Clerical costs for recovery)	Value of orders Number of orders	Value of orders Number of orders	Not allocated
5. *Stock* Amount of stock in warehouse × cost	Value of stock in warehouse servicing the territory	Not allocated (turnover speed?)	Average value of stock per product Notional cost of working capital Space occupied by product in warehouse
6. *Stock control* Planning department staff	Not allocated	Not allocated	Number of inventory postings for product
7. *Advertising* Actual costs, specific to territory or product	Allocated by management	Only when it can be identified with a customer group	Only when it can be identified with a particular product

Only when such a cost analysis is regularly produced can the product manager be held fully responsible for the net contribution of his product. For then he can identify the inputs (costs) of each factor and begin to assess the output (results) of the operation.

For example, he could express objectives for each of the factors in terms of added profitability and best use of resources, eg:

■ Objectives for advertising (outputs):
  - 'To raise the awareness level of potential buyers of the product from 10 per cent to 15 per cent in year 1 within what would be the annual cost of eight salespeople.'
  - 'To double the level of recognition of control improvement benefits among current users before the end of next year within a cost level of €X,000.'
■ Objectives for the salesforce (outputs):
  - 'An increase in revenue of 5 per cent above forecast price levels in the annual invoiced sales figure' (input = product costs).
  - 'To increase the coverage of the chemical industry companies in Territory ABC by 25 per cent by the end of December' (input = territory costs).

Such objectives need to be agreed (of course) with the managers involved. So too does the method of checking:

1. that activities have been performed;
2. that activities have paid off.

The danger he must avoid is the situation where if things have not gone well the solution must be found in trying to improve the quality of what is done rather than questioning the basis. He must always look at the end objective and be prepared to put forward valid and carefully thought through alternatives. This will only work if the communication channels have been established and regularly updated.

COMMUNICATION CHANNELS

A book on effective product management would not be complete without some discussion of communication. Of all the managers in the marketing area of the company the product manager has to communicate with more people – and at greater length – than almost any other.

Table 11.5 shows the major contacts to be made by the product manager in the course of his normal function. Normal contacts with bosses and staff have not been included.

Table 11.5 *Product manager's contacts*

Who	What about	How	How often
Customers	Product benefits Prices Features Availability Reactions	Advertising Direct mail Media advertisements Sales promotion Market research	{ Continuous { process Product launch Six-monthly
Production department	Plans/forecasts } Objectives Resources Specifications } Monitoring	Annual meeting Six-monthly } review } { Monthly meetings { Reports { Ad hoc discussions { Annual review	Once a year Every six months Each month Monthly/quarterly As necessary Per year
Sales department	Targets/ objectives Action	Meetings } Presentations of } benefits } Reports	Before seasonal launches Monthly
Advertising agent	Programme for the season/ year Results	Meetings with account executives Discussion of effectiveness	Six-monthly Monthly
Market research agency	Programme Questionnaire Sample selection Results/reports	Discussion and briefing Meeting	Ad hoc { On presentation { of results
R&D department	Development programmes Technical innovations	Six-monthly 'round tables'	At times set by R&D
Accounting department	Budgets Overhead allocation (see Table 11.4) Results	Reports and memos Figures	During budget preparation Every month

An increasingly popular form of organisation structure is shown in Figure 11.3. This shows the responsibility of the product manager for the 'contribution' of his product across all markets, similarly the responsibility of market managers (sales managers) for 'contribution' of all their customers involved in purchasing all product ranges. This means the involvement of each product manager with each market manager in discussions of the product/market plan – identified by the boxes in the matrix – and in the application for the services of the advertising department or the market research function into one or other of the product/market areas. This repeats Figure 2.2 to demonstrate communication actions.

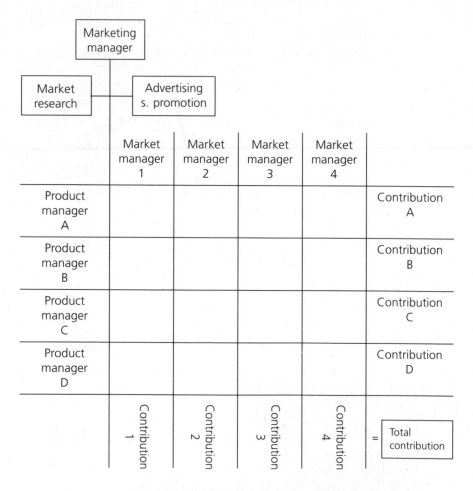

Figure 11.3 *Matrix organisation*

Finally, the product manager needs to perform her function usually without any formal authority except that which she can gain from her own skill, knowledge, enthusiasm and commitment. She needs therefore to be conscientious, patient, persevering and above all persuasive. For he must manage the product from its conception to the hands of the user – and ensure both user satisfaction and product profitability.

CHECKLIST

Communication Instruments

Letters, memos, faxes, e-mails, voicemails

■ What point are you trying to make? (What is your objective? What result do you want? What should the reader or listener do, feel, believe?)
■ The style should fit the recipient (he/she should feel comfortable with it).
■ The person receiving the letter/memo should understand it.
■ Use clear, appropriate and concise wording.
■ Avoid jargon.

Meetings

■ Why is the meeting to be held?
■ Should it be formal or informal?
■ What are the objectives of the meeting?
  – dissemination of information;
  – consultation and feedback;
  – generating new ideas;
  – establishing a plan or procedure;
  – progress monitoring.
■ Plan the time and place of the meeting:
  – establish agenda;
  – invite participants;
  – arrange process recording *(minute taking);*
  – decide on 'flip-chart writer';
  – set time limits for subjects to be discussed;
  – distribute documentation.
■ During the meeting:
  – ensure each person has their 'say';
  – draw out shy people;
  – hold back domineering people;

- keep the subject in mind all the time;
- allow breaks *(coffee, tea, 'cooling off')*
- set dates for next meeting.
■ After the meeting:
  - see that minutes are produced;
  - minutes should identify those who are responsible for 'action';
  - minutes should show agreed deadlines;
  - distribute 'formal' and 'informal' minutes.

Reports

■ Ensure they fit the terms of reference.
■ Check on the purpose of the report. Is it to:
  - record events?
  - describe facts?
  - make judgements?
  - make recommendations?
  - persuade to a course of action?
■ To whom is it to be addressed?
  - her/his position and responsibilities?
  - what sort of person?
  - what use will he/she make of the report?
■ Framework of the report should be as follows:
  - introduction (including terms of reference);
  - summary of proposed action;
■ Benefits of action;
■ Details of action;
■ Background (facts and conclusions);
■ Recommend action.

Personal presentations

■ Make a plan:
  - set out the main points;
  - pick out important ones;
  - stress benefits.
■ Think about the audience:
  - who are they?
  - what do they expect?
  - what are the barriers to the acceptance of your message?
■ Rehearse:
  - practise your presentation;
  - check mechanicals (visuals, overhead projector, etc).

AND FINALLY...

The Product Manager, young or old, male or female, new or experienced, needs three key skills:

■ *analysis* – for examining market trends and picking out likely areas of current and future profitability;
■ *planning* – so as to take account of the resources at his or her disposal and to set them down in a feasible order of priority;
■ *communication* – so that all those within the organisation who are responsible for making the plans work can see the strength of the arguments and co-operate willingly;
and lots of luck!

Now you may read the Preface!

Bibliography

Abell, D F and Hammond, J G (1979) *Strategic Market Planning*, Prentice-Hall, New Jersey.

Anson, C J, unpublished notes for Urwick Management Centre management courses 1965, 1966, 1967.

Baker, M J (1985) *Marketing Strategy & Management*, Macmillan, Basingstoke.

Clewet and Stosch (1972) 'Shifting Role of the Product Manager', *Harvard Business Review*, January–February.

Crouch, S (1985) *Marketing Research for Managers*, Pan Books, London.

Dalla and Yuspeh (1976) 'Forget the Product Life Cycle', *Harvard Business Review*, January-February.

Davidson, J H (1972) *Offensive Marketing*, Cassell, London.

Dominguez, G S (1971) *Product Management*, American Management Association.

Foster, D W (1972) *Planning for Products and Markets*, Longman, London.

Kotler, P (1984) *Marketing Management, Analysis Planning and Control* (5th edition), Prentice-Hall, International, London.

McDonald, M (1989) *Marketing Plans*, Heinemann, London.

O'Shaughnessy, J (1987) *Why People Buy*, Oxford University Press Inc., New York.

Parker, R C (1982) *The Management of Innovation*, John Wiley, London.

Phillips, W (1989) *Confessions of a Marketeer*, Mercury Books, London.

Rickards, T (1982) *Stimulating Innovation*, Frances Pinter, London.

Smith, A (1976) *Inquiry into the Nature and Causes of the Wealth of Nations*, Edinburgh.

Wheatley, M, 'Variable Factor', *Management Today*, February 1989.

White, R (1976) *Consumer Product Development*, Pelican, Hounslow.

Note: There may be later editions of the books mentioned. There will certainly be other articles. These can start you thinking.

Index